S0-DZP-639

How Cellphones Cropped, Distorted, and Visually Censored Cinema: Let's Save Cinema

Copyright © Thecyclecasenumber Goalinventionsystemauthor 2022 All Rights Reserved.

Copyright © Russel Alden Arlotta 2022 All Rights Reserved. Artwork by © Amungwa Linus 2022

Copyrighted officially through The United States of America Copyright Offices, Copyright.Gov

With Painting Scenes by: KAYAMAN Arts Studio (Kaya)

No part of this book may be distributed, recorded, or shared without the written permission from the author.

**Feel free to provide comments, questions, and feedback about this book at my email thecinema3stepsolutionbook@gmail.com**

**Please Note: I do not use any Online Social Media or Online Video accounts. The above email is the only way to contact me regarding this book.**

**Please Note: This book requires to be sold exclusively in its hard cover version, as it was written with narrow margins. The hardcover format allows the insides of all the book's pages to be easily read.**

# How Cellphones

## Cropped,
## Distorted,
## and
## Visually Censored Cinema:

# Let's Save
# Cinema

**Author: Thecyclecasenumber Goalinventionsystemauthor**

**Painter: KAYAMAN from KAYAMAN ARTS Studio**

Greetings  *Iman / Hanan* ,

I hope you enjoy my second and final full-length textbook entitled:

"How Cellphones Cropped, Distorted, and Visually Censored Cinema: Let's Save Cinema"

The "Let's Save Cinema" book is available to buy at the Politics & Prose Bookstore in DC and available to order at the Politics & Prose Bookstore website.

I am also happy to announce that my two books are now available for purchase on the Google Play Store. Click the "Books" section once you get to the Google Play Store, then search "Goal Invention" or "Let's Save Cinema" to find and purchase the eBooks at very affordable prices between $3 and $5.

$5 – Goal Invention: The Mental Therapy, Sport, and Hobby

$3 – How Cellphones Cropped, Distorted, and Visually Censored Cinema: Let's Save Cinema

Would appreciate your purchase and a 5-Star (or any star) review for both books, as it helps the book be found by others as well.

With the completion of both books' physical and digital releases, I have finished the only two books that I wanted to write. However, I'm looking forward to releasing smaller pamphlet-sized productions in the future.

Best and Take Care,

Russel

To: Iman & Hanan
RA 2022 $\frac{29}{45}$

# Acknowledgements:

## Personal Acknowledgements:

I thank my mom, dad, and my sisters for their constant support throughout this project. I thank my friend and colleague Kaya for supporting me throughout this book's production. This book would not have been possible without the support that I received from my friends Kaya, Silas, and Itoikai. I worked on this book during the waiting periods of my first feature length book, *Goal Invention: The Mental Therapy, Sport, and Hobby*. I was able to apply the support systems and resources that I had in place from the first book to help me finish my second book, *How Cellphones Cropped, Distorted, and Visually Censored Cinema: Let's Save Cinema*.

Just like my first book, this book is a credit to the lifetime of support and love from my mom and dad.

## Inspirational Acknowledgements:

I thank Louie Tee from Louie Tee Network Productions. I learned from LT, that content does not have to be perfect, and that the most important aspect of content creation is getting one's message across. I was inspired and instilled with confidence from LT's productions over the last 8 years. This book was a complete unknown when I began this project, and I am happy that I was able to go through the process of content creation and create and complete this book.

## Cinema Acknowledgements:

This book offers constructive criticisms and constructive solutions that benefit both consumers and movie streaming companies like Netflix, Hulu, Prime Video, and Tubi. This book also offers constructive criticisms and constructive solutions that benefit both consumers and Hollywood, Bollywood, and South Indian Cinematic Movie Companies.

I dedicate this book to the Cast and Crew of the thousands of Bollywood, Hollywood, and South Indian Cinematic movies that I enjoyed from 2010-2016. It is the memories of these experiences which constantly drove me to create and finish this book: I created this book so that the current generation and future generations can access, consume, and enjoy cinematic movies in their original contents and original aspect ratios on all devices and applications without the films being cropped, distorted, and visually censored.

Special Thanks: I thank the Politics & Prose Bookstore and the Opus Self-Publishing crew, as they helped me throughout the self-publishing and printing process of this book over the last few seasons.

## Introduction + Book Preview

Cinema was my life for about 6 years. I loved enjoying and experiencing Hollywood, Bollywood, and South Indian Cinematic movies for a span of 6 great years from 2010-2016. I am grateful and privileged to have experienced many amazing emotions and journeys through the artform of cinema. My cinematic life primarily consisted of Bollywood and South Indian Cinematic films, and I would not be exaggerating that most of my greatest experiences in life originated from cinema during those 6 years from 2010-2016. My fondest memories from cinema originated from Bollywood movie companies such as Shemaroo, Rajshri, Eros Entertainment, Ultra Movie Parlour, and many others which I accessed through a multitude of platforms including Netflix, Hulu, Prime Video, and each company's official YouTube channel. After 2016, I noticed that the movies that I loved were being visually censored, cropped, or distorted more and more each year.

At this current time, almost every movie from Hollywood, South Indian Cinema, and Bollywood's 100+ year history is either distorted (junked, morphed, and composted by 50% less in size at the vertical length) or visually cropped/censored (in which 50% of the films' contents are removed at the top and bottom) from the cinematic film. Even the physical DVD versions of old movies are being re-released with the films' contents visually censored/cropped or distorted/morphed/junked. In fact, it is almost impossible for the consumer to access and experience this planet's bibliography of cinematic films in their original contents without the films' contents being severely visually cropped/censored (which removes nearly 50% of films' contents and pixels) or distorted/morphed (in which the films' contents are junked and composted to be 50% less in size).

To see my favorite movies from Hollywood and Bollywood systematically visually censored/cropped or distorted/junked/morphed/composted on movie streaming platforms inspired me to create this book to raise awareness about the issue. I felt that it was my responsibility to apply all the effort that I could, so that future generations of individuals could experience and enjoy the world's amazing cinematic histories, stories, and journeys in the same way that I was fortunate to have experienced. Throughout this book, I address corporations such as Netflix, Hulu, Prime Video, Goldmines, Shemaroo, Eros Entertainment, Ultra Movie Parlour, and YouTube Movie channels out of respect for their services which I enjoyed for many years. I also highlight these companies because this book's purpose is to raise awareness to these companies to allow the global citizen to enjoy cinema from movie streaming platforms on all devices without the content of movies being visually cropped/censored or distorted/morphed/junked/composted. While this book may seem overcritical, I mention these corporations out of respect for the many great years of service they provided up until 2016.

It is important to note that movie streaming corporations such as Netflix, Hulu, Prime Video, and Official YouTube Movie channels like Shemaroo, Ultra Movie Parlor, and YouTube Movies provided excellent services from the origins of digital cinema up until the year 2016. From 2016 onwards, these entertainment and movie streaming companies started to crop/visually censor films by nearly 50%. From 2016 onwards, movie streaming companies also began distorting, morphing, junking, and composting the contents of films to be nearly 50% less in size at the vertical length. I simply highlight companies by name with respect for the purpose of raising awareness about the problem of movie cropping/censorship (which removes nearly 50% of films' contents and pixels) and distortion (the junking and composting of films to be 50% less in size at the vertical length) in order to promote a solution. I hope that individuals can experience and enjoy movies' contents in a visually uncropped/uncensored and undistorted (unjunked and unmorphed) way just as past generations did prior to the year 2016. **Regardless of Opinions and Beliefs, One Thing is Abundantly Clear:**

**The cropping, distortion, and visual censorship of cinematic films are blatant violations of freedom of speech, freedom of media consumption, and the copyright protections of cinematic films.**

# My Primary Purposes of this Book: this Book will Raise Awareness…

1. … that cellphone trends have caused the visual cropping and censorship of most films from Hollywood, Bollywood, South Indian Cinema, and the world by nearly 50% percent. The visual cropping/censorship of cinematic films to the cellphone-aspect ratios (of 19:9-21:9) removes nearly 50% of films contents and pixels.

2. … that cellphone trends have caused the visual distortion, morphing, junking, and composting of many films by distorting films' contents to the cellphone-aspect ratios (of 19:9-21:9) which reduces the size of distorted films' contents and pixels by nearly 50% percent at the vertical length (by junking, morphing, and composting films at the vertical length to be nearly 50% less in size at the vertical length).

3. … about the scientific anatomy of the visual experience of cinema regarding cinema's various aspect ratios from the 4:3 aspect ratio all the way up to the 21:9 aspect ratio. I will review each aspect ratio of cinema as they relate to the standard sight, vision, and field of view of the anatomical human eyes. I will raise awareness that the human eyes see and experience sight in field of views which are most comparable to the aspect ratios of 4:3-16:9. Through my comparisons of the various aspect ratios of cinema, I will establish a clear scientific understanding that the 16:9 and 4:3 aspect ratios offer the best life-like visual immersions, simulations, emotions, and entertaining cinematic experiences at the scientific anatomic level of the field of vision and sight of the human eyes.

4. … about how cellphone trends negatively affect the cinematic experience through the unnecessary visual cropping/censorship of 50% of the original content of most films ever made. I also made this book to raise awareness of how cellphone trends unnecessarily distorted movies to cellphone-aspect ratios which reduces the films' vertical length by 50% (the distortion of cinema to the cellphone-aspect ratios of 19:9-21:9 junks, morphs, and composts films' contents to be 50% less in size at the vertical length).

5. … about my beliefs that It should be a basic right for the global citizen to have freedom of media consumption and have the basic human right of being provided with the freedom, ability, and choice to enjoy, access, and consume cinematic movies in their original contents and original aspect ratios without the contents and pixels of the cinematic movies being forcefully visually censored/cropped or distorted (junked/morphed/composted) by nearly 50%.

   **This Book's Solution: The *Cinema 3-Step Solution*:** I will raise awareness about the *Cinema 3-Step Solution*, a technological solution which solves the issue of movie censorship/cropping and distortion. The *Cinema 3-Step Solution* provides the consumer with freedom of media consumption, honors the principles of cinema copyright, and allows the consumer to watch movies or shows in their original contents & original aspect ratios (Step 1), visually censored/cropped (Step 2), or visually distorted/morphed/junked/composted (Step 3). The *Cinema 3-Step Solution* provides consumers the choice to watch films in their original contents & original aspect ratios and provides consumers the freedom, ability, and choice to visually crop/censor or distort films to fill or fit their devices' screens. This technology is already available and installed in most affordable DVD playing machines and DVD playing applications, so there is no reason why movie streaming companies should continue to forcefully deny consumers freedom of media consumption by needlessly visually censoring/cropping and distorting cinema across all devices and platforms. The solution is there, and it consists of only a few sentences. I hope that the world will recognize that the forced visual censorship/cropping of films is unlawful, unethical, and a basic violation of the principles of freedom of media consumption and copyrights. I hope that the world will recognize that the forced visual distortion of cinematic films to fit ultrawide cellphone-aspect ratios by junking, morphing, and composting the films' contents to be 50% less in size at the vertical length is unlawful, unethical, and a basic violation of freedom of media consumption and the copyright protections of cinematic films.

# Introduction + Book Preview

I hope that the most basic laws will exist at the local, national, and world-wide level to protect and preserve cinematic history by counting the unnecessary forced visual cropping/censorship and distortion (junking and composting) of cinematic films as an illegal act of copyright violation toward the works of the millions of hardworking professionals that created our planet's films across multiple generations. I hope that the most basic laws will exist at many levels to protect and preserve cinematic history by counting the unnecessary forced visual cropping/censorship and distortion of cinematic films as an illegal act simply by the fact that the global (and even paying) citizen is denied freedom of media consumption with the inability to watch a film in its original visually uncropped/uncensored or undistorted/unjunked/uncomposted contents.

A recurrent theme that I will apply throughout this book is that both the forced visual cropping/censorship and the distortion of cinematic movies are violations of freedom as freedom also applies to freedom of media consumption. As consumers of cinema, whether it be Hollywood, Bollywood, South Indian Cinema, or any Cinema genre, we should be able to have the freedom of media consumption to enjoy cinematic films in their original contents & original aspect ratios without the cinematic films being either visually cropped/censored by nearly 50% (which removes nearly 50% of films' contents and pixels) or distorted, morphed, junked, and composted to the cellphone screen-aspect ratios of 19:9-21:9 (which distorts, morphs, junks, and composts the size of films to be 50% reduced at the vertical length).

This simple act of honoring freedom of speech and freedom of media consumption toward the consumer is possible by applying the *Cinema 3-Step Solution*. The *Cinema 3-Step Solution* presents a film in its original uncropped/uncensored or undistorted contents and provides the consumer the freedom, ability, and choice to watch a film or show in its original contents & original aspect ratio (Step 1), visually cropped/censored (Step 2), or visually distorted/morphed/junked/composted (Step 3). The *Cinema 3-Step Solution* is already installed on most bargain DVD players and DVD playing applications, so there is no excuse for movie streaming companies like Prime Video, Hulu, Netflix, Tubi, and Official YouTube Movie Channels to continue to deny the consumer freedom of media consumption by providing the consumer with forced visually censored/cropped and distorted/morphed/junked cinematic films.

Hollywood, Bollywood, South Indian Cinema, Official YouTube Movie Channels, and Movie streaming platforms like Netflix, Prime Video, Hulu, and Tubi are denying consumers the principles of freedom, freedom of speech, freedom of media consumption, and are systematically visually cropping/censoring and distorting/morphing movies (junking and composting films' contents). Hollywood, Bollywood, South Indian Cinema, Official YouTube Movie Channels, and Movie streaming platforms like Netflix, Prime Video, Hulu, and Tubi are violating the principles of freedom of media consumption, as the consumer is forced to watch and consume films that have been severely cropped/censored or distorted (junked, morphed, and composted). The global consumer has no freedom and no ability to experience films without films being visually cropped/censored by nearly 50%. The global consumer has no freedom and no ability to experience films without films being visually distorted, morphed, junked, and composted to the ultrawide cellphone-aspect ratios of 19:9-21:9 (which reduces the size of films' contents and pixels by 50% at the vertically). The denial of freedom and denial of ability to consume and enjoy cinematic movies in their original contents & aspect ratios is a major violation of freedom, freedom of media consumption, and the principles of copyright.

## Introduction + Book Preview

At the ethical level, how is it acceptable to deny consumers the freedom, ability, and choice to access and enjoy movies by forcefully visually censoring/cropping films by 50% or distorting (junking, morphing, and composting) films to be 50% less in size at the vertical length. At the legal level, how can movie streaming companies and movie companies visually crop/censor and distort/morph/junk/compost cinematic films' content. The visual censorship/cropping of cinema is no different than a form of artistic robbery or vandalism, as in most cases half of most films' contents and pixels are entirely removed from the film. Even worse, in the case of cinema distortion, the films' contents and pixels are distorted, morphed, junked, composted, and reduced in size by nearly 50% at the vertical length. The act of cinema distortion to the cellphone-aspect ratios of 19:9-21:9 is no different than taking all the paintings from an art museum and junking, morphing, distorting, and composting each painting to be 50% less in size at the vertical length. At the logical level, it makes no sense to visually crop/censor and distort/junk/morph/compost cinematic films across all devices. Considering how easy it is to install the *Cinema 3-Step Solution* (of which the principles of the solution are already installed on bargain DVD players and bargain DVD playing applications), there is no reason why for streaming companies like Prime Video, Hulu, Netflix, Official Youtube Movie Channels, and Tubi to continue the forced unnecessary visual cropping/censorship and distortion/morphing/junking/composting of cinema.

Whether cinema is in English, Hindi, Tamil, or any language in the world, it should be a basic right of humanity and the laws of copyrights, freedom, freedom of speech, and freedom of media consumption to watch, consume, and experience films the way they were originally created without 50% of the content visually censored, cropped, and removed from the cinematic experience. It also should be a basic right of humanity and the laws of freedom, freedom of speech, and freedom of media consumption to be able to watch cinematic movies in their original contents & original aspect ratios without them being unnecessarily and forcefully distorted to cellphone-aspect ratios (which distorts, morphs, junks, and composts the films' original contents and pixels to be 50% reduced in size at the vertical length).

Cinema is needed more than ever, yet, in 2022 as a global civilization, we are denied basic principles of freedom, copyrights, freedom of speech, and freedom of media consumption. As a global civilization, the global citizen does not have the freedom, choice, or ability to watch movies without 50% of the movies' contents and pixels visually cropped/censored and removed entirely. As a global civilization, the global citizen does not have the freedom, ability, or choice to watch movies without the original films' contents being unnecessarily and forcefully distorted, morphed, junked, and composted to fit cellphone-aspect ratios (which reduces the size of films by nearly 50% at the vertical length).

The visual cropping/censorship and distortion/morphing (junking and composting) of cinema is the "gold standard" and the "cinematic standard" of the entertainment world and movie streaming companies offering Hollywood, Bollywood, and South Indian Cinematic films (Prime Video, Hulu, Netflix, Tubi, Shemaroo, Goldmines, Ultra Movie Parlor, YouTube Movie Channels etc.). What is most inexplicable, inexcusable, and unethical about the "gold standard" of entertainment, is that the cropping/censorship and distortion/junking of cinema is completely unnecessary. There is a simple a solution (the *Cinema 3-Step Solution*) to end the forced visual censorship/cropping and distortion/morphing/junking/composting of cinema which can be explained in a simple brief paragraph.

## Introduction + Book Preview

The solution to end the forced visual censorship/cropping and distortion of cinema is so simple that I will include the solution in this book's introduction:

---

### The *Cinema 3-Step Solution*
### to End the Forced Visual Cropping/Censorship and Distortion of Cinema:

**Step 1:** Provide movies in their original contents & original aspect ratios without visually cropping/censoring or distorting/morphing/junking/composting the films' contents and pixels. *Note:* When a modern cellphone is being used horizontally, it can display films made in every type of cinematic aspect ratio ever made (whether the film is 4:3, 16:9, 18:9, 19.5, or 21:9 aspect ratio) without the film being cropped/censored or distorted in any way as the part of the cellphone screen not being used displays black bars/black spaces/black curtains.

**Step 2:** If the consumer is watching a movie on a cellphone device, the consumer has the freedom, ability, and choice to click "zoom to fill cellphone screen" (which visually crops/censors the film by nearly 50% percent). Alternatively, the cellphone consumer can return to *Step 1* of the *Cinema 3-Step Solution* and watch the movie without the movie being visually cropped/censored.

**Step 3:** If the consumer is watching a movie on a cellphone device, the consumer has the freedom, ability, and choice to click "distort to fit cellphone screen" (which distorts, morphs, junks, and composts a film by reducing the films' size, contents, and pixels by nearly 50% at the vertical length). Alternatively, the cellphone consumer can initiate *Step 1* of the *Cinema 3-Step Solution* or *Step 2* of the *Cinema 3-Step Solution.*

### Freedom of Media Consumption = The *Cinema 3-Step Solution*
### The *Cinema 3-Step Solution* provides the consumer the ability, freedom, and choice to watch a film in its original contents & original aspect ratio (Step 1), to watch a film visually cropped/censored (Step 2), and to watch a film distorted/junked/composted (Step 3).

Note: The *Cinema 3-Step Solution* is already installed on most bargain DVD players and DVD playing applications, so there is no reason why movie streaming companies should deny consumers freedom of media consumption by forcing the visual cropping/censorship of films by nearly 50%. There is no reason why movie streaming companies should continue to apply the forced visual distortion of films (which reduces, morphs, junks, and composts the size of films by nearly 50% less in size at the vertical length). The *Cinema 3-Step Solution* provides the consumer with freedom of media consumption, as the consumer has the freedom, ability, and choice to watch films as they were originally made in their original contents & original aspect ratios (Step 1), visually cropped/censored (Step 2), or visually distorted/junked/morphed/composted (Step 3).

---

I tried my physical DVD players, and I also tried my downloaded DVD player applications for my laptop, and I confirmed that both the physical DVD players and the DVD player applications already apply the *Cinema 3-Step Solution*. Most bargain DVD players and DVD player applications adhere to the principles of freedom of speech, copyrights, and freedom of media consumption by providing the consumer the freedom, ability, and choice to watch a film in its original contents & original aspect ratio (Step 1), the freedom, ability, and choice to "zoom to fill" which crops/visually censors the film's contents (Step 2), and the freedom, ability, and choice to "distort to fill" which distorts/junks/composts/morphs the film's contents (Step 3).

## Introduction + Book Preview

The technology to apply the *Cinema 3-Step Solution* to provide consumers with the freedom of media consumption toward consuming and experiencing cinema has been around for years and is installed on most affordable DVD players and DVD playing applications which were developed by small teams of individuals. It is inexcusable, unethical, and should be illegal for Hollywood, Bollywood, South Indian Cinematic Companies, and movie streaming companies like Netflix, Hulu, Tubi, Prime Video, and Official Youtube Movie channels to continue to deny the consumer freedom of media consumption by forcing the consumer to consume films in a visually cropped/censored or visually distorted (junked and composted) forms.

Hollywood, Bollywood, South Indian Cinematic Companies, and movie streaming companies like Netflix, Hulu, Prime Video, and Tubi continue to unnecessarily force the visual cropping/censorship and distortion/junking/composting of films for no apparent reason other than the domino effect of cellphone market trends. Again, I am singling out specific companies out of respect to raise awareness to those corporations to provide their films in their original contents and allow the consumer the freedom, ability, and choice to watch films in their original contents & aspect ratios (Step 1), visually cropped/censored (Step 2), or visually distorted, junked, morphed, and composted (Step 3). As a consumer in a democracy, you should have the freedom, ability, and choice to watch, experience, consume and enjoy a movie without nearly 50% percent of its visual contents visually censored/cropped. As a consumer in a democracy, you should have the freedom, ability, and choice to watch, experience, consume, and enjoy a movie without the film's contents being morphed, junked, composted, and reduced in size at the vertical length by nearly 50% percent.

As demonstrated by the *Cinema 3-Step Solution* (which is already available in DVD players, videogame systems. and DVD playing applications), the consumer should have the freedom, ability, and choice to access a film's original contents and make the decision themselves to either watch the movie in its original contents & original aspect ratio (uncropped/uncensored and undistorted) (Step 1), to watch the movie visually cropped/censored (Step 2), or to watch the movie's contents morphed and distorted to their device's aspect ratio (Step 3). The *Cinema 3-Step Solution* solves the issue of forced movie cropping/censorship and distortion//morphing/junking/composting uniformly across all devices, applications, and platforms.

Considering how small teams of developers behind most bargain DVD player applications and DVD players already apply the *Cinema 3-Step Solution*, there is no reason for Hollywood, Bollywood, South Indian Cinematic Companies, and movie streaming companies like Netflix, Hulu, Prime Video, Tubi, and Official Youtube Movie channels to continue to deny consumers freedom, freedom of media consumption, experiences, and visual journeys by forcing the visual cropping/censorship of films by 50% at the top and bottom. There is no reason for Hollywood, Bollywood, South Indian Cinematic Companies, and movie streaming companies like Netflix, Prime Video, Tubi, Hulu, and Official YouTube Movie Channels continue to deny consumers freedom of media consumption by forcing the distortion of cinematic movies which junks, morphs, composts, reduces the film's original size by 50% less at the vertical length.

**The *Cinema 3-Step Solution* provides the consumer and global citizen the freedom, ability, and choice to consume and enjoy cinematic films in their original contents & original aspect ratios without the films being visually cropped/censored by 50% or distorted/junked/morphed by 50% less in size.**

## Introduction + Book Preview

The purpose of this book is not only to raise awareness about the visual cropping/censorship and distortion/junking/composting of cinema completed by Hollywood, Bollywood, South Indian Cinematic Companies, and movie streaming companies like Netflix, Hulu, Prime Video, and Tubi: throughout this book, I will provide a scientific anatomical examination of the various aspect ratios of cinema. I will provide lessons which examine and compare which aspect ratios of cinema are entertaining, simulating, and immersive. The efforts of this book are two-fold: I hope that Hollywood, Bollywood, South Indian Cinematic Companies, and movie streaming companies like Netflix, Hulu, Prime Video, and Tubi apply the *Cinema 3-Step Solution*, the solution which ends the forced movie cropping/censorship and distortion/junking of cinema by providing consumers the freedom, ability, and choice to watch cinema which follows the principles of the *Cinema 3-Step Solution* ((Original Contents & Original Aspect Ratios (Step 1), Visually Cropped/Censored (Step 2), or Visually Distorted/Junked (Step 3)). The *Cinema 3-Step Solution* is already installed on most DVD players and DVD playing applications, so it will be very easy for movie streaming companies to honor and comply with copyrights, freedom, freedom of speech, and freedom of media consumption to consumers & world citizens.

I also hope to educate and raise awareness that both native films and films that are visually cropped/censored or distorted/junked to the cellphone-aspect ratios of 19:9-21:9 provide non-immersive, non-simulating, and non-enjoyable experiences at the scientific anatomic level of human vision. This is due to the fact that the standard vision of the human eye sees in an aspect ratio (or field of view) which is between the 16:9 and 4:3 aspect ratios. The aspect ratios of 19:9-21:9 are in fact unnatural, unrealistic, non-life like visual field of views as they cut off the field of view of normal sight by nearly 50% percent. To no surprise, most glasses and sunglasses are made in an aspect ratio between the 16:9 and 4:3 aspect ratios. We experience sight and life in an aspect ratio (or field of view) somewhere between the 16:9 aspect ratio and the 4:3 aspect ratio. Furthermore, each of our eyes experience sight and field of vision between the 16:9 and 4:3 aspect ratios.

When we watch movies that are either native, visually cropped/censored, or distorted/junked/morphed/composted to the 19:9-21:9 cellphone-aspect ratios, our minds can tell the difference, as we know that the 19:9-21:9 aspect ratios provide unrealistic, non-life-like, non-immersive, non-simulating-limited visual field of views, non-entertaining simulations, and non-enjoyable cinematic experiences. The cellphone-aspect ratios of 19:9-21:9 only simulate half of the field of view of the standard vision and sight that the human eyes experience real life in.

We experience movies the same way we experience life: the key to immersion, entertainment, and simulation in cinema is to watch movies in aspect ratios which mimic and simulate how we see the world in real life with our own eyes. When we watch movies in aspect ratios (16:9 to 4:3 aspect ratios) that are similar to the field of views we visually experience sight in real life, we feel amazing life-like immersions, experiences, simulations, and the euphorias of entering other cinematic worlds. The 19:9-21:9 cellphone-aspect ratios at the scientific anatomical levels are in fact anti-cinema, as those aspect ratios defeat the purpose of cinema. The 19:9-21:9 aspect ratios at the scientific anatomical levels of human sight offer limited non-immersive, non-simulative, non-cinematic, non-entertaining, and most importantly non-enjoyable cinematic experiences. The purpose of cinema is to enjoy life by having a great cinematic experience and to enter and experience cinematic worlds: The ultrawide aspect ratios of 19:9-21:9 offer no immersions, no simulations, no entertainment, and do not initiate the phenomenon of the visual euphoric experiences of cinema. Cinematic films both native, cropped/visually censored, or distorted/junked to the 19:9-21:9 aspect ratios are contraindicative to the very definition of the word "cinema".

<u>Introduction + Book Preview</u>

**The standard field of vision of the human eye sees life in aspect ratios between the 16:9-4:3 aspect ratios.**

## The Anatomical Aspect Ratios (or Field of Views) of Human Vision: The 4:3-16:9 Aspect Ratios

1. I kindly request you to close one of your eyes, to look around, and to think if the vision of your eye was displayed on a television screen, what aspect ratio would it be.
2. I kindly request you to open your eyes, to close your other eye, to look around, and to think if the vision of your eye was displayed on a television screen, what aspect ratio would it be.
3. I kindly request you to open both your eyes, with both your eyes open, look around, and think if your vision was displayed on a television screen, what aspect ratio would it be.
4. The majority of the answers should be between the 16:9 and 4:3 aspect ratios. The cellphone 19:9-21:9 aspect ratios are not found within the standard field of vision of humanity.

*Note A:* When we watch movies and shows that are displayed in the 16:9 to 4:3 aspect ratios, we are immersed in the experience, we feel the experience, we enter other worlds, and we enjoy cinematic movies... This is because movies that are shown in aspect ratios which simulate the standard field of vision of the human eyes (the 4:3-16:9 aspect ratios) cause life-like cinematic immersions, as our minds cannot tell the difference between real worlds and cinematic worlds. Films displayed in the 4:3-16:9 aspect ratios simulate the aspect ratios we experience field of vision in real life which tricks the human mind to experience the film just as we experience real life. I term this effect as the visual euphoria of cinema.

*Note B:* When we watch movies and shows that are displayed in the 19:9-21:9 cellphone-aspect ratios, we are half immersed in the experience, we are only half simulated, and we never quite enter and experience those movie worlds. This is because movies that are shown in the cellphone-aspect ratios of 19:9-21:9 only simulate 50% of the field view we experience vision at the anatomical level in real life. The 19:9-21:9 aspect ratios do not simulate the standard field of vision in which we visually experience real life (the anatomical vision of the human eye is somewhere between the 16:9 and 4:3 aspect ratios). Films displayed in the 19:9-21:9 aspect ratios simulate only half the field of view we experience field of vision in real life. When we watch films in the 19:9-21:9 aspect ratios, the human mind is not tricked, as the field of view is nearly 50% less from what we experience real life in. The phenomenon of visual euphoria, visual simulation, and visual immersion of cinema does not occur because the brain is not tricked by limited field of view aspect ratios like the 19:9-21:9 aspect ratios. The 19:9-21:9 aspect ratios at the scientific anatomical level provide limited non-enjoyable visual immersions, limited non-enjoyable cinematic experiences, limited non-enjoyable immersions, and limited non-enjoyable simulations.

*Conclusion:* Cinematic movies displayed in the 19:9-21:9 aspect ratios offer unrealistic, non-immersive, non-simulative, non-entertaining, non-euphoric, and non-enjoyable experiences at the scientific anatomic level of human vision. Cinematic movies displayed in the 16:9-4:3 aspect ratios offer life-like realistic, immersive, simulative, entertaining, euphoric, and enjoyable visual experiences which simulate the way our eyes see and experience field of vision in real life.

**It is well established at the anatomical level of human sight that cinematic content presented in the 19:9-21:9 aspect ratios are significantly less enjoyable, less immersive, less simulative, less life-like, and less entertaining than films presented in the 16:9-4:3 aspects ratios ((the 4:3-16:9 aspect ratios mimic and simulate the aspect ratio (or field of view) of standard human sight)).**

## The Visual Euphoria, Visual Simulation, and Visual Immersion of Cinema

The key to experiencing the emotions of joy, happiness, romance, comedy, and excitement of cinema is to experience cinema which mimics how we see real life in. We see real life in an aspect ratio (or field of view) which resembles between the 16:9 and 4:3 aspect ratios. Cinematic movies either native, visually cropped/censored, or distorted/morphed/junked to the 19:9-21:9 aspect ratios create limited non-enjoyable, non-simulative, non-euphoric, and non-immersive experiences. The 19:9-21:9 cellphone-ultrawide aspect ratios are unnatural aspect ratios and quite opposite to the standard vision (and field of view) we experience life in (our eyes experience sight somewhere between the 16:9 and 4:3 aspect ratios). The 19:9-21:9 aspect ratios only simulate about half of the field of vision that we experience sight in.

Cinema both native, visually cropped/censored, or distorted (junked and composted) to the 19:9-21:9 aspect ratios provide non-realistic, non-immersive, and non-simulating visual experiences which provide limited emotions of joy, happiness, romance, comedy, entertainment, and excitement at a significantly reduced level from a scientific anatomical perspective. The secret to happiness, emotions, entertainment, and escapes into other cinematic worlds lies within the aspect ratios of our eyes (the field of view that the human eyes experience sight) and the screens we experience cinema. The "visual euphoria" of cinema only occurs with cinema that is made in aspect ratios (4:3-16:9) that simulate the way we experience sight at the anatomical level of the human eyes (the 4:3-16:9 aspect ratios simulate the standard field of view that the human eyes see and experience sight). The phenomenon of the "visual euphoria, visual simulation, and visual immersion" of cinema results from the phenomenon that the mind cannot tell the difference between real life and cinema.

Cinema which is made in aspect ratios which simulate the way we experience and see real life (16:9 to 4:3 aspect ratios) provide realistic, life-like, immersive, and simulating visual experiences which creates the phenomenon of a "visual euphoric experience". The visual euphoria of cinema can be best described as being transported into the cinematic world that you are watching. The visual euphoria, visual simulation, and visual immersion of cinema occurs from watching cinematic films displayed in aspect ratios which simulate the vision (the field of view of standard sight) we experience life in (4:3-16:9 aspect ratios).

From the scientific anatomic level of vision, cinematic films presented in the 19:9 to 21:9 aspect ratios are scientifically unable to create the phenomenon of the visual euphoria of cinema. This is because the mind can tell the difference between cinematic content provided in life-like aspect ratios that our eyes experience sight in (4:3- 16:9) and cinematic films displayed in the cellphone-aspect ratios of 19:9-21:9 (the 19:9-21:9 aspect ratios simulate about 50% of the field of view of standard sight and human vision). Cinematic films displayed in the cellphone-aspect ratios of 19:9-21:9 simulate about only 50% of how we experience sight in real life, and as a result the human mind is unable to be tricked into cinematic immersion or cinematic simulation. The mind can tell the difference between cinematic films that are presented in life-like aspect ratios that simulate the standard field of view of the human eyes (16:9 to 4:3 aspect ratios) and cinematic films displayed in unrealistic limited field of view aspect ratios (19:9-21:9 aspect ratios) which simulate about only 50% of the standard sight (field of view) of the human eyes.

Conclusion: The 19:9-21:9 cellphone-aspect ratios do not cause the visual euphoria, visual simulation, and visual immersion of cinema, as they are not able to at the scientific anatomical level of the human eyes. The 4:3-16:9 aspect ratios cause the visual euphoria, visual simulation, and visual immersion of cinema as they simulate the way we see and experience real life in at the scientific anatomical level of the human eyes.

**Sight (4:3-16:9) + Screens (4:3-16:9) = Visual Euphoria, Immersion, and Simulation of Cinema**
**Sight (4:3-16:9) + Screens (19:9-21:9) = No Euphoria, No Immersion, and No Simulation of Cinema**
**The key to experiencing the visual euphoria of cinema is to watch cinema the way our eyes see in real life.**

To conclude my introduction, I want to restate that the purpose of this book is to promote freedom and freedom of media consumption by creating laws around the world which follow the *Cinema 3-Step Solution* and allow the consumer and the global citizen the freedom, ability, and choice to watch movies in their original contents & original aspect ratios (Step 1), visually cropped/censored "zoom to fill" (Step 2), or visually distorted/composted/junked/morphed "distort to fit" (Step 3) across all their devices. The inability for humanity to watch a film without nearly 50% of the film visually cropped/censored from the experience is an inexcusable violation of freedom, freedom of media consumption, and the principles of copyright law. The inability for humanity to watch a film without the film being distorted, morphed, junked, and composted by nearly 50% at the vertical length is an inexcusable violation of freedom, freedom of media consumption and the principles of copyright law. The *Cinema 3-Step Solution* ends the forced visual censorship/cropping and distortion/morphing/junking of cinema uniformly across all devices, applications, and platforms and honors the principles of copyrights, freedom, freedom of speech, and freedom of media consumption.

The primary purpose of this book is to teach and explain the *Cinema 3-Step Solution*; however, I also include my hopes, beliefs, experiences, and dreams about cinema throughout this book.

# End of Introduction.

# End of Introduction.

# Table of Contents

## Chapter 1: How Cellphones Visually Cropped/Censored and Distorted Cinema

I was fortunate enough to experience and enjoy 1000's of Cinematic Hollywood, Bollywood, and South Indian Cinematic movies in my life (from 2010-2016) before the 50% percent visual censorship/cropping of cinema was initiated by movie-streaming platforms and became the "gold standard" or "Cinematic Standard" of movie streaming companies like Netflix, Hulu, Prime Video, Tubi, and Official Youtube Movie Channels (Shemaroo, Goldmines, Ultra Movie Parlor). I was also very fortunate to experience Hollywood, Bollywood, and South Indian Cinematic Movies in their original contents & original aspect ratios before they were distorted, junked, morphed, composted, and reduced by 50% percent in size at the vertical length by movie streaming companies. When I return to watch my favorite Hollywood, Bollywood, and South Indian Cinematic movies, I am heartbroken and in disbelief to see that nearly 50% percent of the films I loved have been visually cropped/censored and removed from the experience. I am also heartbroken and in disbelief to see my favorite movies distorted, junked, morphed, and reduced in size by nearly 50%.

In both cases, the experience of watching a movie that has been visually censored/cropped or distorted/junked/morphed/composted is unwatchable, non-entertaining, non-immersive, upsetting and a non-enjoyable experience. It is heartbreaking to see the works of generations and generations of millions of hardworking film makers, cast, actors, and crews work to be to either visually censored/cropped and removed by nearly 50% or distorted, junked, composted, and morphed unnecessarily to the ultrawide cellphone-aspect ratios to be nearly 50% less in size at the vertical length. I believe that the forced visual cropping/censorship and distortion/junking/composting of cinema is unbelievable, unethical, unlawful, un-professional, and violates the principles of copyrights, freedom, freedom of speech, and freedom of media consumption. The feelings that I experience to know that the thousands of amazing movies from Hollywood, Bollywood, and South Indian Cinema that I enjoyed have been unnecessarily censored/cropped and distorted/morphed/junked/composted by cellphone trends is what drove me to create this book. What I could not get beyond, is how could such a reality exist, and how could such a blatant violation of copyrights, freedom, freedom of speech, and freedom of media consumption occur from companies whose jobs it is to provide cinema to consumers.

The answer to how cellphones visually cropped, censored, and distorted cinema is the domino effect induced by cellphone trends. The forced and unnecessary visual censorship/cropping and distortion/junking/morphing/composting of cinema initiated by Hollywood, Bollywood, South Indian Cinematic Companies, official YouTube Movie Channels, and movie streaming companies (like Netflix, Hulu, Prime Video, Tubi) exists for no other reason than to follow the domino effect of forcing consumers to watch films significantly visually censored/cropped and distorted/junked/morphed/composted. Netflix was one of the first leading movie streaming companies to begin the domino effect of movie censorship/cropping and distortion/junking/morphing/composting. Following the domino effect of visual censorship/cropping and distortion/composting of cinema heavily started by Netflix, other movie streaming companies such as Hulu, Prime Video, and Tubi, all fell in line with the domino effect.

**The phenomenon of just wanting to fit in with domino effect of cellphone trends is why cinematic companies deny consumers and global citizens freedom & freedom of media consumption by either visually censoring/cropping cinematic movies or distorting/junking/morphing/composting films into the cellphone-aspect ratios of 19:9-21:9, which reduces the size of films by 50% at the vertical length.**

## Chapter 1: How Cellphones Visually Cropped/Censored and Distorted Cinema

Hollywood, Bollywood, South Indian Cinematic Companies, and movie streaming companies like Netflix, Hulu, Prime Video, Tubi visually censor/crop and distort/junk/morph/compost most cinematic films for no other reason other than following the market domino effect of cropping, distortion, and visual censorship. The domino effect of the visual censorship/cropping and distortion/junking/morphing/composting of cinema began when movie streaming companies like Netflix, Prime Video, Hulu, and Tubi started to think that cinema in the cellphone-aspect ratios of 19:9 and 21:9 is trendy (as those are the aspect ratio of cellphones) therefore, the movie streaming companies took it upon themselves to visually censor/crop and distort/junk/morph/compost nearly every movie ever made, across all applications and devices and violate movie copyrights and deny consumers freedom & freedom of media consumption by visually censoring/cropping films by 50% and distorting/composting/junking cinematic films by 50% less in size.

It is important to remember that cellphones trends do not change the fact that these Hollywood, Bollywood, South Indian Cinematic companies, Official YouTube Movie Channels, and movie streaming companies (Netflix, Hulu, Prime Video, Tubi) violate movie copyrights and deny consumers freedom & freedom of media consumption by committing visual censorship/cropping and distortion/junking/morphing/composting of all the movies that we love in this world for no other reason than falling in line with the domino effect Induced by cellphone trends. It is important to remember that the forced visual censorship/cropping and distortion/junking/morphing of cinema induced by cellphone market trends is completely unnecessary as demonstrated by the *Cinema 3-Step Solution.*

## The *Cinema 3-Step Solution* to End the Market Domino Effect of the Forced Visual Cropping/Censorship and Distortion of Cinema Induced by Cellphone Trends:

**Step 1:** Provide movies in their original contents & original aspect ratios without visually cropping/censoring or distorting/junking/morphing/composting the films' contents and pixels. The freedom, ability, and choice to access, consume, and enjoy a movie in its original contents & original aspect ratio should be a basic right of humanity, freedom, and copyrights.
*Note:* When a modern ultrawide cellphone is being used horizontally, it can display films made in every type of cinematic aspect ratio ever made (whether the film is displayed in the 4:3, 16:9, 18:9, 19:9, or 21:9 aspect ratio) without the film being cropped/censored or distorted/junked/composted/morphed in any way as the part of the cellphone screen not being used displays black bars/black spaces/black curtains.

**Step 2:** If the consumer is watching a movie on a cellphone device, the consumer has the freedom, ability, and choice to click "zoom to fill the cellphone screen" (which visually crops/censors the film by nearly 50% percent). Alternatively, the cellphone consumer can initiate *Step 1* of the *Cinema 3-Step Solution* and watch the movie without the movie being visually cropped/censored.

**Step 3:** If the consumer is watching a movie on a cellphone device, the consumer has the freedom, ability, and choice to click "distort to fit cellphone screen" (which unnaturally distorts, morphs, junks, and composts a film's original size and contents by reducing the films size by nearly 50% at the vertical length). Alternatively, the cellphone consumer can initiate *Step 1* of the *Cinema 3-Step Solution* or *Step 2* of the *Cinema 3-Step Solution.*

## Chapter 1: How Cellphones Visually Cropped/Censored and Distorted Cinema

The phenomenon of how cellphones censored/cropped and distorted/junked/morphed/composted cinema can be best explained by the domino effect of cellphone market trends. The absolute unnecessary situation of cinema's visual censorship/cropping and distortion/composting originated after the first movie streaming company started the process. Now, no matter what platform you wish to see your movie on, whether it is Netflix, Hulu, Prime Video, Tubi, or any entertainment company's official YouTube channel (such as Shemaroo, Ultra Movie Parlor, Gold Mines etc.), you will most likely be forced to watch and experience the movie you wish to see with nearly half of the film's visual contents cropped/censored (or even worse, you will be forced to watch the movie distorted/junked/composted/morphed by 50% less in size vertically).

Once the first domino fell, all the other entertainment companies fell in line with the industry "gold standard" of cinema's visual cropping/censorship, and distortion/junking/morphing/composting. The complete disregard for copyrights, freedom, freedom of speech, and freedom of media consumption exhibited by Hollywood, Bollywood, South Indian Cinematic Movies, Official Youtube Movie channels, and movie streaming companies like Netflix, Hulu, Prime Video, and Tubi is what inspired me to create this book. I believe it is time for the most basic principles of freedom, freedom of media consumption, copyrights, and ethics to end the forced visual cropping/censorship and distortion/junking/composting/morphing of cinema across Hollywood, Bollywood, South Indian Cinema, official YouTube Movie channels, Netflix, Hulu, Prime Video, and Tubi by applying the *Cinema 3-Step Solution* (which is already installed in most DVD players and DVD playing applications). The *Cinema 3-Step Solution* is a solution which provides the consumer the freedom, ability, and choice to watch films in their original contents & original aspect ratios (Step 1), to visually crop/censor "zoom to fill cellphone screen" films (Step 2), or to visually distort/junk/morph/compost "distort to fit cellphone screen" films (Step 3) (which junks, composts, and reduces the size of films' contents and pixels by 50% at the vertical length).

If small teams of individuals can apply the principles of the *Cinema 3-Step Solution* on bargain DVD players and DVD player applications, there is no reason for Hollywood, Bollywood, South Indian Cinema, and movie streaming companies like Netflix, Hulu, Prime Video, Tubi, and Youtube Movie Channels to continue to deny consumers freedom and freedom of media consumption by unnecessarily and forcefully visually censoring/cropping films by nearly 50% or by visually distorting, junking, morphing, and composting films by 50% at the vertical length.

## Freedom of Speech & Media Consumption = The *Cinema 3-Step Solution*

## The *Cinema 3-Step Solution* provides the consumer the ability, freedom, and choice to watch a film in its original contents & original aspect ratio (Step 1), to watch a film visually cropped/censored (Step 2), and to watch a film distorted/junked/morphed/composted (Step 3). End of Chapter 1.

## Chapter 2: Focus on the Positives and Potentials of Cinema to End the Forced Visual Cropping/Censorship and Distortion/Junking/Morphing/Composting of Cinema.

The name of Chapter 2 is the answer to the question, "why should we care that the domino effect induced by cellphone trends has visually censored/cropped cinema by nearly 50% or distorted/junked/morphed/composted cinema by 50% less in size at the vertical length?"

### The Answer is Simple:

**Focus on the positives and potentials of being able to enjoy your favorite cinematic movies without them being visually cropped/censored by nearly 50% or distorted/junked/composted by nearly 50% less in size at the vertical length.**

- Can you imagine how amazing the experiences, joys, and emotions would be to watch movies on movie streaming applications on your OLED 2k-4k HD TV, AMOLED 2k-4k Phone, AMOLED 2k-4k Tablet, or 2k-4k Desktop Monitor without nearly 50% percent of the films' pixels and contents visually censored/cropped?

- Can you imagine how amazing the experiences, joys, and emotions would be to watch movies on movie streaming applications on your OLED 2k-4k HD TV, AMOLED 2k-4k Phone, AMOLED 2k-4k Tablet, or 2k-4k Desktop Monitor in their original contents & original aspect ratios, without the films being visually distorted, junked, morphed, composted, and reduced in size by nearly 50% percent at the vertical length?

- Can you imagine how beautiful this planet's amazing Hollywood, Bollywood, South Indian Cinema, and World cinematic films would appear across all your modern devices (with 2k-4k Resolution and stunning AMOLED and OLED screens) in their original contents & original aspect ratios without nearly 50% percent of the films' visual contents and pixels being visually cropped/censored?

- Can you imagine how beautiful this planet's amazing Hollywood, Bollywood, South Indian Cinema, and World cinematic films would appear across all your modern devices (with 2k-4k Resolution and stunning AMOLED and OLED screens) stunning screens in their original contents & original aspect ratios without the films' visual contents and pixels being visually distorted, junked, morphed, composted, and reduced in size by nearly 50% percent at the vertical length?

- Can you imagine the emotions, the happiness, the comedy, the thrills, the romance, and the feelings of immersion into other worlds that cinema would provide, if we were able to watch movies in their original creations on our beautiful modern screens without the films' original contents being censored/cropped by nearly 50% or distorted/junked/morphed/composted to be 50% less in size.

- Can you imagine being able to watch movies in their original contents and original aspect ratios (4:3-16:9 aspect ratios, the aspect ratios which we see and experience the standard field of vision and sight in real life) on our beautiful modern Ultra HD, AMOLED, and OLED screens.

# Focus on the Positives and Potentials of Cinema
# To End the Forced & Unnecessary Visual Cropping/Censorship and Distortion/Junking/Morphing/Composting of Cinema.

## Chapter 2: Focus on the Positives and Potentials of Cinema to End the Forced Visual Cropping/Censorship and Distortion/Junking/Morphing/Composting of Cinema Continued.

All it takes is one actor, actress, crew member, or director from Hollywood, Bollywood, and South Indian Cinema to speak up against the forced and unnecessary visual cropping/censorship and distortion/junking/morphing/composting of cinematic films. All it takes one actress, actor, crew member, or director to raise awareness of the fact that *Bargain DVD players and DVD player applications provide the consumer with the freedom, ability, and choice to watch a film in its original contents & original aspect ratio (Step 1), cropped/visually censored (Step 2), or visually distorted/junked/morphed/composted (Step 3): There is no reason or excuse why moving streaming companies (like Netflix, Hulu, Prime Video, Tubi, and official YouTube Movie Channels) cannot apply the Cinema 3-Step Solution to their movie applications.*

# Can You Imagine...?

-Can you imagine if art museums censored, cut, and removed 50% percent of every painting
(at the top and bottom of each painting) ever painted?

-Can you imagine if art museums distorted, junked, morphed, and composted every painting to be reduced in size by nearly 50% percent at the vertical length?

-Can you imagine if libraries censored and removed 50% percent (at the top and bottom of each page) of the pages of every book in public libraries?

-Can you imagine if libraries distorted, junked, morphed, and composted every book in the public library to be 50% percent less in size at the vertical length?

-Can you imagine if the music industry censored and removed 50% percent of every song ever made?

For all those hypothetical situations, there would be outrage, legal fines, and jail time for most parties and individuals involved, as such circumstances are blatantly obvious acts of vandalism and clear violations of freedom, freedom of speech, freedom of media consumption, and copyrights.

**All of the above examples are blatantly obvious acts of vandalism and clear violations of freedom, freedom of speech, freedom of media consumption, and copyrights.**
**The situation regarding the visual cropping/censorship and distortion/cropping/morphing/junking of cinematic films initiated by Companies like Netflix, Hulu, Prime Video, Tubi, and Official Youtube Movie channels is no different than the hypothetical solutions listed above.**
**Movie streaming companies violate the principles of copyrights, freedom, and freedom of media consumption by forcefully visually censoring/cropping films by 50% or by distorting/junking/morphing/composting films to be 50% less in size at the vertical length.**

**Chapter 2: Focus on the Positives and Potentials of Cinema to End the Forced Visual Cropping/Censorship and Distortion/Junking/Morphing/Composting of Cinema Continued.**

To Hollywood, Bollywood, South Indian Cinematic Companies, and Movie Streaming Companies such as Netflix, Hulu, Prime Video, Tubi, and official YouTube Movie Channels such as Shemaroo, Goldmines, Ultra Movie Parlour, and YouTube Movies, I express this message:

**Focus**

**On**

**The**

**Positives**

**Freedom**

**Of**

**Media**

**Consumption**

Can you imagine how amazing it would be to use and enjoy the movie streaming services of Netflix, Hulu, Prime Video, Tubi, and Youtube Movie channels if the movies that we watched were not visually cropped/censored by nearly 50% or visually distorted/junked/morphed/ composted to be 50% less in size at the vertical length?

Can you imagine how amazing it would be to use and enjoy the movie streaming services of Netflix, Hulu, Prime Video, Tubi, and Youtube Movie Channels if the movies that we watched were in their original uncropped/uncensored and undistorted/unjunked/unmorphed/uncomposted contents and original aspect ratios on our modern beautiful Ultra 2k-4k Resolution-AMOLED, OLED, and LCD screens on all our modern devices (Phones, Tablets, Laptops, Desktops, Televisions Etc.)

**Freedom of Media Consumption and Copyrights Protection = The _Cinema 3-Step Solution_**

**The _Cinema 3-Step Solution_ provides the consumer the ability, freedom, and choice…**

**…to watch a film in its original contents & original aspect ratio (Step 1),**

**…to watch a film visually cropped/censored (Step 2),**

**…and to watch a film distorted/morphed/junked/composted (Step 3).**

# End of Chapter 2.
# End of Section 1.

Use this page to take notes on Section 1.

## Section 2: Lessons

Lesson 1: Experience

Lesson 2: How and Why did Cellphones Crop, Distort, and Visually Censor Cinema?

Lesson 3: A Representation of the Visual Cropping/Censorship and Distortion of Cinema

Lesson 4: Cinema in the 16:9-4:3 aspect ratios + the standard field of vision of the human eyes (16:9-4:3)

Lesson 5: Cinema in the 19:9-21:9 aspect ratios + the standard field of vision of the human eyes (16:9-4:3)

Lesson 6: The *Cinema 3-Step Solution*

Lesson 7: How Cellphones Cropped, Distorted, and Visually Censored Movies on YouTube

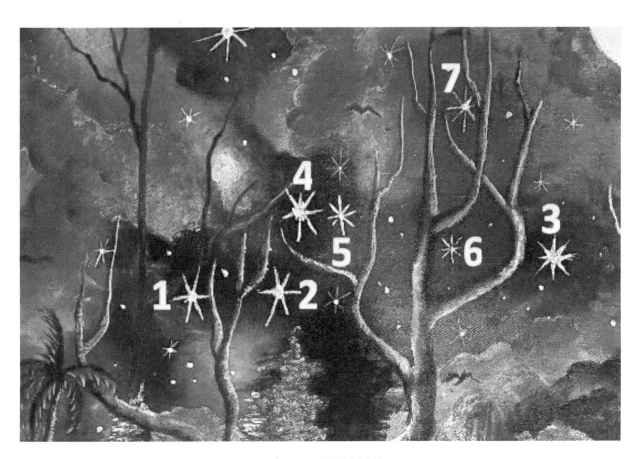

**Painter: KAYAMAN**

## Lesson 1: Experience

Why do we watch movies?

What is the purpose of watching movies?

What is the point of cinema?

The answer is experience

The act of visually cropping/censoring cinematic films to fit the ultra-wide cellphone-aspect ratios of 19:9-21:9 removes nearly 50% percent of the experience (and removes nearly 50% of the films' visual pixels). The act of visually distorting/composting/morphing/junking cinematic films to fit cellphone-aspect ratios unnecessarily distorts, morphs, junks, composts, and reduces the films' experiences at the vertical length by nearly (and distorts, junks, morphs, and composts the films' contents and pixels to be nearly 50% less in size at the vertical length).

We watch movies for experience, and the visual cropping/censorship of cinema by nearly 50% removes nearly half of the original experience. The purpose and point of cinema is to enjoy cinematic films in their original contents and original aspect ratios to experience visual euphorias, immersions, and simulations.

I urge the movie streaming entertainment world such as Netflix, Hulu, Amazon Prime Video, Tubi, Hollywood, South Indian Cinematic Companies, and Bollywood Entertainment companies like Shemaroo Entertainment, Eros Entertainment, Goldmines, and Ultra Movie Parlor to think about one word:

# Experience

Experience is what cinema is all about. The ability for the consumer and global citizen to access, consume, watch, and enjoy movies on online streaming applications across all devices without the content being visually cropped/censored by nearly 50% or distorted/morphed/composted to be nearly 50% less in size at the vertical length is crucial to create a cinematic experience which provides freedom of media consumption. The freedom, ability, and choice for a consumer to access, consume, and enjoy a cinematic movie in its original contents & aspect ratios should be a basic right of humanity, copyrights, and freedom media consumption.

### In the Modern World of the Movie Cropping/Visual Censorship Initiated by Movie Streaming Companies:

We only get to experience 50% percent of the original film director's vision

We only get to experience 50% percent of the original film's sceneries

We only get to experience 50% percent of the original film's emotions

We only get to experience 50% percent of the original film's contents and pixels

### In the Modern World of the Movie Distortion/Morphing/Composting Initiated by Movie Streaming Companies:

We only get to experience the film director's vision after the film has been distorted/junked/composted by 50%

We only get to experience the original film's sceneries after the film has been distorted/junked/composted by 50%

We only get to experience the original film's emotions after the film has been distorted/junked/composted by 50%

We only get to experience the original film's contents after the film has been distorted/junked/composted by 50%

The purpose and point of cinema is not to crop, distort, and visually censor cinema across all devices and applications just to fit in and fall in line with the domino effect of cellphone trends.

The purpose and point of cinema is not to violate copyrights, freedom, and freedom of media consumption.

The purpose and point of cinema is to enjoy cinematic films in their original contents & original aspect ratios to cause visual euphorias, simulations, immersions, and escapes for enjoyable cinematic experiences.

Lesson 1: Experience Continued.

# Freedom of Media Consumption + Experience Is a Beautiful Thing, End The Forced Visual Cropping/Censorship and Distortion/Junking/Morphing/Composting of Cinematic films

# Think About it & Apply

## the *Cinema 3-Step Solution* *(across all devices & applications)*

**Summary:** Consumers deserve the most basic right of freedom of media consumption to experience movies in their original contents & original aspect ratios. Consumers deserve to have the ability, freedom, and choice to experience movies in their original contents and original aspect ratios (Step 1), to visually crop/censor films by nearly 50% "zoom to fill cellphone screen", or to visually distort/junk/morph/compost films to be nearly 50% percent less in size at the vertical length "distort to fit cellphone screen" (Step 3).

Why needlessly deny freedom of media consumption and force the visual cropping/censorship of the world's cinematic experiences by nearly 50% percent across all devices such as televisions, desktops, laptops, cellphones, and tablets, just to fit in with the domino effect induced by cellphones.

Why needlessly deny freedom of media consumption and force the visual distortion, junking, morphing, and composting of the world's cinematic experiences by nearly 50% percent less in size at the vertical length across all devices such as televisions, desktops, laptops, cellphones, and tablets, just for the sake of fitting in with the domino effect induced by cellphones.

It should be a basic right of humanity for the global citizen to have the freedom, ability, and choice to experience a cinematic film in its visually uncropped/uncensored and undistorted/unmorphed/unjunked/uncomposted contents.

## Lesson 2: How and Why did Cellphones Crop, Distort, and Visually Censor Cinema?

**Question:** How and Why did Cellphones Crop, Distort, and Visually Censor Cinema?

**Answer:** Once cellphones transitioned to the cellphone 19-21:9 aspect ratios, movie streaming applications and movie streaming channels such as Netflix, Hulu, Amazon Prime Video, Tubi, and official Youtube movie Channels from Bollywood, Hollywood, and South Indian Cinema thought that It would be a trendy idea to visually crop/censor all of the existing cinematic films' content to the cellphone-aspect ratios of 19:9-21:9 which visually crops/censors cinema by nearly 50%. Even worse, some movie streaming providers thought it would be a trendy idea to visually distort, junk, morph, compost, and reduce the size of films by 50% at the vertical length.

While I understand the domino effect which caused the visual cropping, censorship, and distortion of cinema, the reality of the situation is that movie streaming companies are blatantly violating the principles of freedom, freedom of media consumption, and copyrights by denying the consumer the freedom, ability, and choice to consume and enjoy cinematic movies in their original contents and original aspect ratios.

**Solution:** The *Cinema 3-Step Solution* provides the consumer with the freedom, ability, and choice to consume and enjoy cinematic movies in their original contents and original aspect ratios (Step 1), to visually crop/censor cinematic movies by nearly 50% "zoom to fill cellphone screen" (Step 2), and to visually distort/junk/morph/compost cinematic movies at the vertical length to be nearly 50% less in size "distort to fit cellphone screen" (Step 3). The *Cinema 3-Step Solution* is already installed on most bargain DVD players and DVD playing applications, so there is no excuse for movie streaming companies such as Netflix, Hulu, Prime Video, Tubi, YouTube Movie Channels, and Hollywood, Bollywood, and South Indian Cinematic companies to continue to deny the consumer freedom & freedom of media consumption.

When it is virtually impossible for the global citizen to access this planet's bibliography of films in their original contents and original aspect ratios, then it becomes vital to acknowledge that the global citizen is denied the freedom, ability, and choice of media consumption (which is a violation of freedom). It is important to remember, that just because a trend is trendy, does not mean that it is not a violation of the principles of copyright, freedom, freedom of speech, and freedom of media consumption. The domino effect of cellphone trends does not give movie streaming companies the right and legal permission to deny consumers the choice, ability, and freedom to access, consume, and enjoy cinematic films in their original contents and original aspect ratios.

Chapter 1: Lesson 3: A Representation of the Visual Cropping/Censorship and Distortion of Cinema

Consider the aspect ratios of cinematic movies as windows (or field of views) into other worlds. Below is the 16:9 aspect ratio (top) and the 4:3 aspect ratio (bottom). The majority of movies that you will see on Netflix, Hulu, Tubi, Prime Video, and YouTube were originally made in either the 4:3 aspect ratio or they were made in the 16:9 aspect ratio. The window and field of view to experience cinematic worlds is best simulated by the 4:3-16:9 aspect ratios, as those aspect ratios simulate the way we see, experience sight, and experience field of views in real life. The standard field of vision of the anatomic eye is somewhere between the 4:3 aspect ratio and the 16:9 aspect ratio. When we watch films in the 4:3-16:9 aspect ratios, the visual euphoria, visual immersion, and visual simulation of cinema takes place because our minds cannot tell the difference between what is real and what is not real (because our eyes see field of vision in real life in the 4:3-16:9 aspect ratios).

# 16:9 Aspect Ratio Movie

Note: Most films that are featured on movie streaming companies such as Netflix, Prime Video, Hulu, Tubi, and Official Youtube Movie channels were originally filmed and created in either the 16:9 aspect ratio or the 4:3 aspect ratio.

# 4:3 Aspect Ratio Movie

Note: Most films that are featured on movie streaming companies such as Netflix, Prime Video, Hulu, Tubi, and Official Youtube Movie channels were originally filmed and created in either the 16:9 aspect ratio or the 4:3 aspect ratio.

Chapter 1: Lesson 3: A Representation of the Visual Cropping/Censorship and Distortion of Cinema Continued.

Due to the domino effect induced by cellphone trends, the movie streaming world (Netflix, Hulu, Prime Video, Tubi, Youtube Movie Channels) visually cropped/censored and removed nearly 50% of the visual experience from most of the movies that were ever made. Even worse, the movie streaming world, decided to visually distort, junk, compost, and morph cinematic films to the cellphone-aspect ratios of 19:9-21:9 by reducing the size of films at the vertical length by nearly 50%.

This is a visual representation of the visual cropping/censorship and distortion/composting/morphing/junking of cinema for 16:9 aspect ratio films on movie streaming applications initiated by movie streaming companies such as Netflix, Hulu, Prime Video, Tubi, and Youtube Movie channels

## How Films Created in the 16:9 Aspect Ratio Appear on Movie Streaming Applications such as Netflix, Prime Video, Hulu, Tubi, and Youtube Movie Channels.

# Visually Cropped/Censored

# Or Distorted

# (Morphed/Junked/Composted)

# Visually Cropped/Censored

**At the time of writing this page, consumers using movie streaming platforms are forced to watch movies either cropped/visually censored by 50% or distorted/junked/composted/morphed by 50% to be 50% less in size: These are blatant violations of copyrights, freedom, and freedom of media consumption.**

Chapter 1: Lesson 3: A Representation of the Visual Cropping/Censorship and Distortion of Cinema Continued.

This is a visual representation of
the visual cropping/censorship and distortion/junking/morphing/composting of cinema
for 4:3 aspect ratio films on movie streaming applications
Initiated by movie streaming companies such as Netflix, Hulu, Prime Video, Tubi, and Youtube Movie channels

## How Films Created in the 4:3 Aspect Ratio Appear on Movie Streaming Applications such as Netflix, Prime Video, Hulu, Tubi, and Youtube Movie Channels.

| |
|---|
| Visually Cropped/Censored |
| Or Distorted (Morphed/Junked/Composted) |
| Visually Cropped/Censored |

**At the time of writing this page, consumers using movie streaming platforms are forced to watch movies either cropped/visually censored by 50% or distorted/junked/composted/morphed by 50% to be 50% less in size: These are blatant violations of copyrights, freedom, and freedom of media consumption**

Lesson 4 Cinema in the 16:9-4:3 aspect ratios + the standard field of vision of the human eyes (16:9-4:3)

Humans experience life through sight and fields of viision which can be compared to the field of views on screens termed, aspect ratios. The standard vision that humanity sees the world in is somewhere between the 16:9 and 4:3 aspect ratios. When we consume and enjoy cinematic content displayed in the 4:3-16:9 aspect ratios, visual euphoria, visual simulation, and visual immersion occurs (as cinematic films presented in the 4:3-16:9 aspect ratios simulate the standard human sight's field of view/field of vision).

4:3-16:9 Aspect Ratio Movies + Standard Aspect Ratios of Human Sight (4:3-16:9) = visual euphoria, visual immersion, visual simulation, and immersive life-like & enjoyable experiences into other worlds.

1. We have established that the 4:3 and 16:9 aspect ratios of cinema are most comparable to the aspect ratios which the human eyes see vision, field of views, and experience real life in.

2. The combination of the standard aspect ratio of human sight (16:9-4:3) in combination with a movie experience displayed in the 16:9-4:3 aspect ratios, simulates the natural human field of vision which tricks the brain and causes the phenomenon of visual euphoria, visual immersion, visual simulation, enjoyable experiences, and emotions of cinema.

3. Cinematic films that are displayed in the 4:3 – 16:9 aspect ratios simulate the standard field of vision of the human eyes (the 4:3-16:9 aspect ratios) and offer lifelike, immersive, simulative, entertaining, and euphoric windows into experiencing the cinematic worlds of movies.

# The Math is Simple:

# Sight (4:3-16:9 FOV) + Screens (4:3-16:9 FOV) = Visual Euphoria, Immersion, and Simulation of Cinema

# Sight (4:3-16:9 FOV) + Screens (19:9-21:9 FOV) = No Euphoria, No Immersion, and No Simulation of Cinema

Note: FOV means Field of View/Field of Vision

# The key to enjoying the visual experience, visual simulation, and visual immersion of cinematic movies is to watch cinema the way our eyes see in real life.

Lesson 4 Cinema in the 16:9-4:3 aspect ratios + the standard field of vision of the human eyes (16:9-4:3)

```
┌─────────────────────────────┐
│                             │
│    Cinema 16:9 Aspect       │
│    Ratio (16:9 FOV)         │
│                             │
└─────────────────────────────┘
```

```
     Human Eye                Human Eye
   Vision Aspect            Vision Aspect
       ratio                    ratio
    16:9--4/3 FOV           16:9--4/3 FOV
```

Note: FOV means Field of View/Field of Vision

Cinematic films displayed in the 16:9-4:3 aspect ratios activate and simulate the standard workings of the average human eye's aspect ratio of vision or field of vision which causes:

Visually euphoric, simulative, immersive, and enjoyable cinematic experiences into cinematic worlds.

The standard vision of the human eyes see and experience sight, field of views, and field of vision in real life in an aspect ratio somewhere between the 16:9 and 4:3 aspect ratios.

When we watch cinematic movies that are also in the same aspect ratios of the standard human field of vision (16:9 – 4:3 aspect ratios), immersion, simulation, euphoria, and enjoyable cinematic experiences occur.

```
┌─────────────────────┐
│                     │
│    Cinema 4:3       │
│   Aspect Ratio      │
│    (4:3 FOV)        │
│                     │
└─────────────────────┘
```

Human Eye
Vision Aspect
ratio
16:9--4/3 FOV

Human Eye
Vision Aspect
ratio
16:9--4/3 FOV

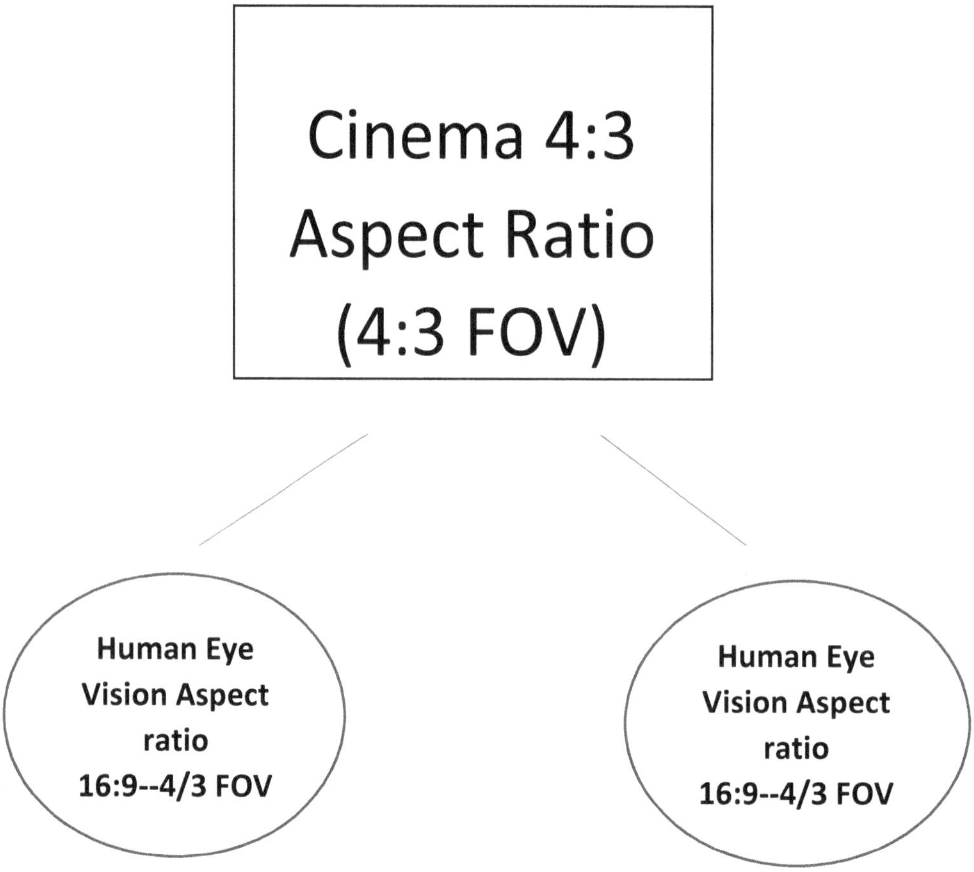

Note: FOV means Field of View/Field of Vision

Cinematic films displayed in the 16:9-4:3 aspect ratios activate and simulate the standard workings of the standard human eye's aspect ratio (or field of vision) which causes
visually euphoric, simulative, immersive, and enjoyable cinematic experiences into cinematic worlds.
The standard vision of the human eyes see and experience sight, field of views, and field of vision in real life in an aspect ratio somewhere between the 16:9 and 4:3 aspect ratios.

Lesson 5: Cinema in the 19:9-21:9 aspect ratios + the standard field of vision of the human eyes (16:9-4:3)

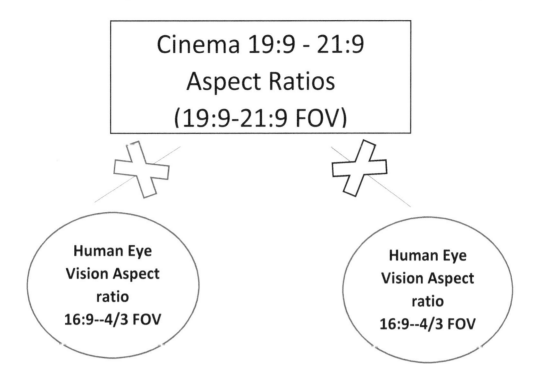

Note: FOV means Field of View/Field of Vision

Cinematic films displayed in the 19:9-21:9 aspect ratios do not activate and do not simulate the normal workings of the standard human eye's aspect ratio of vision (or field of vision) which causes:

A non-immersive, non-simulative, non-lifelike, non-enjoyable, and visually limited experiences into cinematic worlds.

**The standard field of vision of the human eyes see and experience life in an aspect ratio somewhere between the 16:9 and 4:3 aspect ratios. When we watch cinema that is either natively made, cropped/visually censored, or distorted/junked/morphed/composted to the cellphone-aspect ratios of 19:9-21:9, limited non-immersive, non-simulative, non-lifelike, non-enjoyable, non-euphoric, and limited visual experiences occur.**

Cinematic movies displayed in the 19:9-21:9 cellphone-aspect ratios provide non-enjoyable visual experiences. The 19:9-21:9 aspect ratios **do not cause** the visual euphoria, visual simulation, and visual immersion of cinema, as the mind cannot simulate the standard field of vision of the human eyes (the 4:3-16:9 aspect ratios). In other words, the mind cannot be tricked into being immersed and simulated in the film, because cellphone 19:9-21:9 aspect ratio films provide limited field of view-visual experiences. The cellphone aspect ratios of 19:9-21:9 activate and simulate only 50% of the standard sight and field of vision of the human eyes. The cellphone-aspect ratios of 19:9-21:9 activate and simulate only 50% of sight, and as a result, at the scientific anatomic level, cause non-immersive, non-simulative, non-lifelike, non-entertaining, non-euphoric, and non-enjoyable visual experiences.

Lesson 5 Continued

Cinematic films in the 19:9-21:9 aspect ratios + the standard field of vision of the human eyes (16:9-4:3)

The combination of the 19:9-21:9 aspect ratios and the standard human field of vision (4:3-16:9 aspect ratios) cause limited non-immersive, non-simulative, non-euphoric, non-entertaining, and non-enjoyable cinematic experiences at the scientific anatomical level of human sight and the human eyes. The 19:9-21:9 aspect ratios are not aligned with the aspect ratios (4:3-16:9) which the human eyes experience sight, field of views, and field of vision in real life, for the human eyes' field of view sees life somewhere between the 16:9 and 4:3 aspect ratios.

**In many ways the 19:9-21:9 aspect ratios are anti-cinematic, anti-immersive, anti-simulative, and non-enjoyable aspect ratios, because they simulate about only 50% of the field of view and sight that the standard vision of the human eyes see and experience real life in.**

We experience cinema no differently than the way we experience real life (through the sight and vision of our eyes), and that is why the principle of the screen's aspect ratio as being the primary vessel and method of being teleported into enjoying cinematic worlds is so important for the immersion, simulation, and entertainment of experiencing life-like enjoyable cinematic experiences into other worlds.

Lesson 6: The *Cinema 3-Step Solution*.

The solution to end the forced visual censorship/cropping and distortion of cinema.

---

# The *Cinema 3-Step Solution*
# to End the Forced Visual Cropping/Censorship and Distortion of Cinema:

**Step 1:** Provide movies in their original contents & original aspect ratios without visually cropping/censoring or distorting/morphing/junking/composting the films' contents and pixels. *Note:* When a modern cellphone is being used horizontally, it can display films made in every type of cinematic aspect ratio ever made (whether the film is 4:3, 16:9, 18:9, 19.5, or 21:9 aspect ratio) without the film being cropped/censored or distorted in any way as the part of the cellphone screen not being used displays black bars/black spaces/black curtains.

**Step 2:** If the consumer is watching a movie on a cellphone device, the consumer has the freedom, ability, and choice to click "zoom to fill cellphone screen" (which visually crops/censors the film by nearly 50% percent). Alternatively, the cellphone consumer can return to *Step 1* of the *Cinema 3-Step Solution* and watch the movie without the movie being visually cropped/censored.

**Step 3:** If the consumer is watching a movie on a cellphone device, the consumer has the freedom, ability, and choice to click "distort to fit cellphone screen" (which distorts, morphs, junks, and composts the film's size, contents, and pixels by nearly 50% at the vertical length). Alternatively, the cellphone consumer can initiate *Step 1* of the *Cinema 3-Step Solution* or *Step 2* of the *Cinema 3-Step Solution.*

# Freedom of Media Consumption = The *Cinema 3-Step Solution*
# The *Cinema 3-Step Solution* provides the consumer the ability, freedom, and choice to watch a film in its original contents & original aspect ratio (Step 1), to watch a film visually cropped/censored (Step 2), and to watch a film distorted/junked/composted (Step 3).

Note: The *Cinema 3-Step Solution* is already installed on most bargain DVD players and DVD playing applications, so there is no reason why movie streaming companies should deny consumers freedom & freedom of media consumption by forcing the visual cropping/censorship of films by nearly 50%. There is no reason why movie streaming companies should continue to apply the forced visual distortion of films (which reduces, morphs, junks, and composts the size of films by nearly 50% less in size at the vertical length). The *Cinema 3-Step Solution* provides the consumer with freedom of media consumption, as the consumer has the freedom, ability, and choice to watch films as they were originally made in their original contents & original aspect ratios (Step 1), visually cropped/censored (Step 2), or visually distorted/junked/morphed/composted (Step 3).

Lesson 7: How Cellphones Cropped, Distorted, and Visually Censored Movies on YouTube

Unfortunately, cellphone trends and the domino effect of cellphone trends and "just wanting to fit in" goes beyond cinema and extends to the company YouTube and Online Videos. I would be remiss if I did not include a lesson in this book addressing this issue, as the *Cinema 3-Step Solution* fixes the situation of cropping, distortion, and visual censorship on YouTube as well. For this purpose, I have modified the solution's name to the *YouTube Video 3-Step Solution*.

When I look back at my memories from before 2016, I enjoyed many movies and world music videos on YouTube. At the time of writing this page in 2022, the majority of all movies, music videos, and videos from content creators on YouTube have been cropped/visually censored by 50% or distorted/junked/morphed/composted by 50% to be nearly 50% less in size at the vertical length. It breaks my heart to see my favorite movies, music videos, and videos from content creators as the majority of the videos I consumed and enjoyed have been cropped/visually censored by 50% or distorted/junked/composted/morphed to be nearly 50% less in size vertically. These violations of freedom, freedom of media consumption, freedom of speech exist for no other reason then YouTube falling in line with the domino effect of cellphone trends and just wanting to fit in.

The cropping/visual censorship and distortion/junking/composting/morphing that YouTube has performed is a blatantly obvious violation of copyrights, freedom of speech, and freedom of media consumption. The ability to watch and enjoy a video (I.E a movie) on YouTube in its original contents & original aspect ratio without the video (I.E a movie) being cropped/visually censored by 50% or distorted/junked/cropped/morphed should be a basic right of freedom, freedom of speech, and freedom of media consumption in a democracy. The complete violation of copyrights and freedom of media consumption exhibited by YouTube towards content creators and YouTube consumers is as inexplicable as the cropping, distortion, and visual censorship performed by movie streaming companies like Netflix, Hulu, Prime Video, and Tubi.

The blatant violation of copyrights, freedom, and freedom of media consumption provided on the platform of YouTube to content creators and consumers is inexcusable. In 2022, as a consumer, it is practically impossible to watch and enjoy videos in their original contents & aspect ratios without the video being cropped/visually censored by 50% to "fit in and fall in line with the domino effect of cellphones". In 2022, as a consumer, it is practically impossible to watch and enjoy videos in their original contents & original aspect ratios without the videos being distorted, junked, morphed, and composted by 50% (which reduces the size of videos to be 50% less in size vertically) for no other reason than "falling in line with domino effect of just wanting to fit in with cellphone domino effect".

The consumer and global citizen has practically no freedom and no freedom of media consumption. The ability to access, consume, watch, and enjoy a video (let's say a movie a or a music video) on YouTube, without the video being cropped/censored by 50% should be a basic right of humanity, copyrights, freedom, and freedom of media consumption. The ability to watch and enjoy a video (let's say a movie or a music video) on YouTube without the video being cropped/distorted/junked/morphed to be 50% less in size, should be a basic right of copyrights, freedom, freedom speech, and freedom of media consumption.

Lesson 7: How Cellphones Cropped, Distorted, and Visually Censored Movies on YouTube

One of the benefits of life is that life can be enjoyed. There are many music videos, movies, and videos from content creators that can be enjoyed on YouTube. The choice, freedom, and ability to enjoy videos on YouTube in their original contents & original aspect ratios should be a basic right of freedom, copyrights, and freedom of media consumption.

YouTube has cropped, distorted, and visually censored the online video platform & experience across all devices such as tablets, cellphones, laptops, desktop monitors, and televisions for no other reason than falling in line with the domino effect of cellphone trends. It is important to remember that just because an act is trendy, does not make it any less a blatant violation of copyrights, freedom, freedom of speech, and freedom of media consumption.

The *Cinema 3-Step Solution* not only solves the problem of cropping, distortion, and visual censorship of cinema, but it also solves the issue on YouTube. For this situation, I have modified the name of the solution to be the *YouTube Video 3-Step Solution*. This simple solution provides the consumer and global citizen the ability, freedom, and choice to watch a video (let's say a movie or music video) on YouTube in its original contents & original aspect ratio (Step 1), to watch a video on YouTube cropped/visually censored to fill their cellphone screen "zoom to fill" (Step 2), and to watch a video on YouTube distorted/morphed/junked/composted to fit their cellphone screen "distort to fit" (Step 3).

If bargain DVD Player applications and DVD players which were made by small teams of individuals can apply the principles of the *YouTube Video 3-Step Solution*, then there is no excuse or reason for the YouTube company to continue to deny consumers and content creators of the most basic rights of copyrights, freedom, freedom of speech, and freedom of media consumption.

One of the benefits of life is that life can be enjoyed. There are many music videos, movies, and videos from content creators that can be enjoyed on YouTube. The choice, freedom, and ability to enjoy videos on YouTube in their original contents & original aspect ratios without the videos being cropped/visually censored by 50% or distorted/junked/morphed/composted to be 50% less in size (vertically) should be a basic right of humanity, freedom, copyrights, and freedom of media consumption.

Lesson 7: How Cellphones Cropped, Distorted, and Visually Censored Movies on YouTube

## The *YouTube Video 3-Step Solution*

**The *YouTube Video 3-Step Solution*
to End the Forced Visual Cropping/Censorship and Distortion of Videos and Content Creators on YouTube:**

**Step 1:** Provide videos on YouTube in their original contents & original aspect ratios without visually cropping/censoring or distorting/morphing/junking/composting the videos contents and pixels. *Note:* When a modern cellphone is being used horizontally, it can display videos made in every type of cinematic aspect ratio ever made (whether the video is 4:3, 16:9, 18:9, 19.5, or 21:9 aspect ratio) without the video being cropped/censored or distorted in any way as the part of the cellphone screen not being used displays black bars/black spaces/black curtains.

**Step 2:** If the consumer is watching a video on YouTube on a cellphone device, the consumer has the freedom, ability, and choice to click "zoom to fill cellphone screen" (which visually crops/censors the video by nearly 50% percent). Alternatively, the cellphone consumer can return to *Step 1* of the *YouTube Video 3-Step Solution* and watch the video without the video being visually cropped/censored.

**Step 3:** If the consumer is watching a video on YouTube on a cellphone device, the consumer has the freedom, ability, and choice to click "distort to fit cellphone screen" (which distorts, morphs, junks, and composts a video's original size and contents by reducing the video's size, contents, and pixels by nearly 50% at the vertical length). Alternatively, the cellphone consumer can initiate *Step 1* of the *YouTube Video 3-Step Solution* or *Step 2* of the *YouTube Video 3-Step Solution.*

**Freedom of Media Consumption = The *YouTube Video 3-Step Solution*
The *YouTube Video 3-Step Solution* provides the consumer the ability, freedom, and choice to watch a video in its original contents & original aspect ratio (Step 1), to watch a video visually cropped/censored (Step 2), and to watch a video distorted/junked/composted (Step 3).**

Note: The principles of the *YouTube Video 3-Step Solution* are already installed on most bargain DVD players and DVD playing applications, so there is no reason why YouTube should deny consumers freedom of media consumption by forcing the visual cropping/censorship of videos by nearly 50%. There is no reason why YouTube should continue to apply the forced visual distortion of videos (which reduces, morphs, junks, and composts the size of videos by nearly 50% less in size at the vertical length). The *YouTube Video 3-Step Solution* provides the consumer with freedom of media consumption, as the consumer has the freedom, ability, and choice to watch videos as they were originally made in their original contents & original aspect ratios (Step 1), visually cropped/censored (Step 2), or visually distorted/junked/morphed/composted (Step 3).

Lesson 7: How Cellphones Cropped, Distorted, and Visually Censored Movies on YouTube

# End of Lesson 7.

# End of Section 2.

# Section 3:

# The

# *Cinema 3-Step Solution*

# In Action

## Section 3: The *Cinema 3-Step Solution* in Action (Let's Save Cinema)

In Section 3, I will present and evaluate 9 fictional movie scenes in 9 separate films as they apply the *Cinema 3-Step Solution*. Section 3 will consist of 3 parts which will simulate the 3 respective steps of the *Cinema 3-Step Solution.* The final portion of Section 3 will include a comparative conclusion for you to evaluate and notice the differences of the 9 films' 9 scenes in their original aspect ratios & contents, cropped/visually censored contents, and distorted/junked/morphed/composted contents as they apply the *Cinema 3-Step Solution*.

**Note:** The painting scenes in Section 3 originate from the painting which KAYAMAN custom made for my full-length interactive textbook, *Goal Invention: The Mental Therapy, Sport, and Hobby*. The painting scenes selected have been used with permission from KAYAMAN. I had many plans on how to illustrate both the visual cropping/censorship and distortion of cinema and the *Cinema 3-Step Solution,* but once I returned to studying Kaya's painting, I knew that there were more solutions, inspirations, and resources from Kaya's painting that I could use to show the *Cinema 3-Step Solution* in action. I thank Kaya for his painting and support which helped me throughout both the full-length textbook, *Goal Invention: The Mental Therapy, Sport, and Hobby* (222 pages reader interactive textbook) and this book.

## Part 1:                                Step 1 of the *Cinema 3-Step Solution*

In part 1, I will display 9 fictional movie scenes from 9 fictional movies, which follow Step 1 of the *Cinema 3-Step Solution* in which the films' contents are displayed in their original contents and their original 4:3-16:9 aspect ratios. Step 1 of the *Cinema 3-Step Solution* is an example of Hollywood, Bollywood, South Indian Cinematic Companies, movie streaming companies (like Netflix, Prime Video, Hulu, Tubi), and Official YouTube Movie channels providing consumers the freedom, ability, and choice to access, consume, and enjoy films in their original contents and original aspect ratios (without any cropping/visual censorship and without any distortion/morphing/junking/composting).

## Part 2:                                Step 2 of the *Cinema 3-Step Solution*

In part 2, I will display 9 fictional movie scenes from 9 fictional movies which follow Step 2 of the *Cinema 3-Step Solution* in which the films' contents are cropped/visually censored by nearly 50%. Step 2 of the *Cinema 3-Step Solution* is an example of Hollywood, Bollywood, South Indian Cinematic Companies, and movie streaming companies (like Netflix, Prime Video, Hulu, Tubi) and Youtube Movie channels providing consumers the freedom, ability, and choice to consume films cropped/visually censored to fill ("zoom to fill cellphone screen") their cellphones' screens (which crops/visually censors nearly 50% of the films' contents.

## Part 3:                                Step 3 of the *Cinema 3-Step Solution*

In part 3, I will display 9 fictional movie scenes from 9 fictional movies which follow Step 3 of the *Cinema 3-Step Solution* in which the films' contents are distorted, junked, and composted by nearly 50% less in size at the vertical length (the films' contents and pixels are junked, morphed, and composted to be nearly 50% less in size). Step 3 of the *Cinema 3-Step Solution* is an example of Hollywood, Bollywood, South Indian Cinematic Companies, and movie streaming companies (like Netflix, Prime Video, Hulu, Tubi) and Official YouTube Movie channels providing  consumers the freedom, ability, and choice to consume films distorted to fit ("distort to fit") their cellphones' screens (which distorts, junks, and composts the films' contents and pixels to be nearly 50% less vertically).

**Comparative Conclusions I** will present the 9 fictional movie scenes in a collection for you to compare and evaluate each scene as they progress seamlessly through the *Cinema 3-Step Solution*.

# Step 1 of

# The *Cinema 3-Step Solution*

## to End the Forced Visual Cropping/Censorship and Distortion of Cinema:

**Step 1:** Provide movies in their original contents & original aspect ratios <u>without</u> visually cropping/censoring or distorting/morphing/junking/composting the films' contents and pixels.

*Note:* When a modern cellphone is being used horizontally, it can display films made in every type of cinematic aspect ratio ever made (whether the film is the 4:3, 16:9, 18:9, 19.5, or 21:9 aspect ratio) without the film being cropped/censored or distorted in any way as the part of the cellphone screen not being used displays black bars/black spaces/black curtains.

# Step 1 of The *Cinema 3-Step Solution*

**Section 3 Part 1**                    **Step 1 of the Cinema 3-Step Solution**

Step 1 *Cinema 3-Step Solution* in Action    4:3-16:9 Original Aspect Ratio Movie Scene 1

**Movie Scene 1**: A documentary about the moon which shows beautiful footage of the moon.

*Original Movie Aspect Ratio 4:3-16:9*

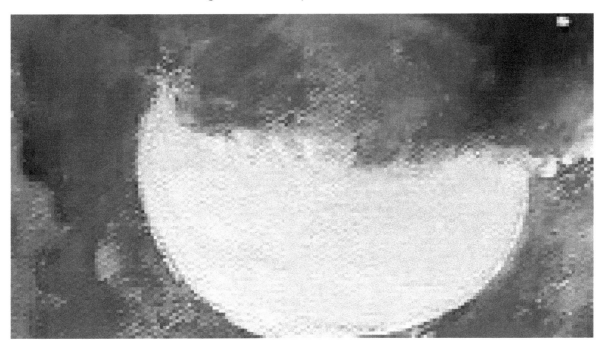

Step 1 *Cinema 3-Step Solution* in Action    4:3-16:9 Original Aspect Ratio Movie Scene 2

**Movie Scene 2**: A documentary about a beautiful constellation of stars that can only be seen a few days each year.                    *Original Movie Aspect Ratio 4:3-16:9*

*Section 3 Part 1*          *Step 1 of the Cinema 3-Step Solution*

Step 1 *Cinema 3-Step Solution* in Action   4:3-16:9 Original Aspect Ratio Movie Scene 3

**Movie Scene 3**: A science fiction movie where the lead character shows the village where she grew up.

*Original Movie Aspect Ratio 4:3-16:9*

Step 1 *Cinema 3-Step Solution* in Action   4:3-16:9 Original Aspect Ratio Movie Scene 4

**Movie Scene 4**: A movie about a small-town community that holds its river as its vital source of energy and identity.          *Original Movie Aspect Ratio 4:3-16:9*

Step 1 *Cinema 3-Step Solution* in Action    4:3-16:9 Original Aspect Ratio Movie Scene 5

**Movie Scene 5**: A woman from the city retires from her work and changes her lifestyle to be in a beautiful forest full of greens and trees.      *Original Movie Aspect Ratio 4:3-16:9*

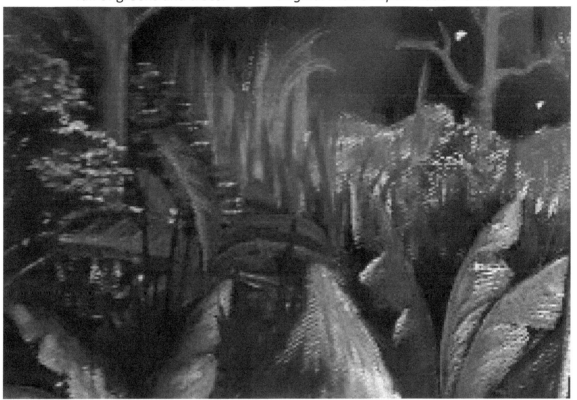

Step 1 *Cinema 3-Step Solution* in Action    4:3-16:9 Original Aspect Ratio Movie Scene 6

**Movie Scene 6:** A young man ponders the future while lying down and looking at the night sky.

*Original Movie Aspect Ratio 4:3-16:9*

Step 1 *Cinema 3-Step Solution* in Action    4:3-16:9 Original Aspect Ratio Movie Scene 7

**Movie Scene 7**: A nature program about a rare type of tree that exists in only certain parts of the world.

*Original Movie Aspect Ratio 4:3-16:9*

Step 1 *Cinema 3-Step Solution* in Action    4:3-16:9 Original Aspect Ratio Movie Scene 8

**Movie Scene 8**: An animated movie of the life a bird that explores the lands, the stars, the forests, and the world

*Original Movie Aspect Ratio 4:3-16:9*

*Section 3 Part 1*          *Step 1 of the Cinema 3-Step Solution*

Step 1 *Cinema 3-Step Solution* in Action    4:3-16:9 Original Aspect Ratio Movie Scene 9

ovie Scene 9: A movie which shows the lifestyle of an old man who tells his life adventures next to the river.

*Original Movie Aspect Ratio 4:3-16:9*

Conclusion:

Step 1 of the *Cinema 3-Step Solution* offers the consumer the freedom, ability, and choice to consume cinematic films in a visually uncropped/uncensored and undistorted manner. The ability to watch films in their original contents and in their original aspect ratios should be a basic right of humanity & freedom, a basic right of freedom of speech & media consumption, and a basic right of copyright protection for all cinematic films created. The fact that the global citizen and consumer is denied the ability to enjoy cinematic films in their original uncropped/visually uncensored or undistorted/unjunked/uncomposted contents is a blatant failure of movie streaming companies such as Netflix, Hulu, Tubi, Prime Video, Official Youtube Movie Channels, the FCC, local, and national governments that continue to deny the world freedom & freedom of media consumption and continue to violate the principles of the copyright protections of cinematic films.

The majority of the world's cinematic films were originally created in the 16:9-4:3 aspect ratios, as those aspect ratios provided the most enjoyable lifelike simulations, immersions, and euphoric visual experiences which simulate the standard sight and field of view of the human eyes. The visual euphoria, visual simulation, and visual immersion of cinema originates from watching cinema which is displayed in the same aspect ratios (or field of views) which the human eyes see and experience sight and field of vision in real life.

# Step 2 of

# The *Cinema 3-Step Solution*

## to End the Forced Visual Cropping/Censorship and Distortion of Cinema:

**Step 2:** If the consumer is watching a movie on a cellphone device, the consumer has the freedom, ability, and choice to click "zoom to fill cellphone screen" (which visually crops/censors the film by nearly 50% percent). Alternatively, the cellphone consumer can return to *Step 1* of the *Cinema 3-Step Solution* and watch the movie without the movie being visually cropped/censored.

# Step 2 of

# The *Cinema 3-Step Solution*

Step 2 *Cinema 3-Step Solution* in Action-4:3-16:9 Aspect Ratio Movie Scene 1 visually cropped/censored by 50%

**Movie Scene 1**: A documentary about the moon which shows beautiful footage of the moon.
*Original Movie Aspect Ratio 4:3-16:9*

Step 2 *Cinema 3-Step Solution* in Action      4:3-16:9 Aspect Ratio Movie Scene 1 visually cropped/censored by 50%

This movie scene has been cropped/visually censored to the cellphone aspect ratios of 19:9-21:9. In the process of cropping/censoring this film's fictional scene, nearly half of the purple clouds are removed from the entire experience. The moon is significantly censored and as such is no longer a moon at the structural level. The moon is now a bodily planet that has the top and bottom removed from the film. Nearly 50% of this movie's scene has been cropped/visually censored and removed entirely from the film: this is a blatant violation of freedom, freedom of speech, freedom of media consumption, and copyrights.

Note: If a museum's paintings were cropped/visually censored by 50%, there would be outrage, fines, and jail times to all parties and individuals involved. The cropping/visual censoring of cinematic movies by 50%, is no different a crime then cropping/visually censoring the paintings of a museum by 50%. At the bare minimum, movie streaming companies like Netflix, Hulu, Prime Video, Tubi, and YouTube Movie Channels should provide the consumer with the freedom, ability, and choice (Step 2 of the *Cinema 3-Step Solution*) for the consumer to choose to crop/visually censor "zoom to fill cellphone screen" the cinematic films that the consumer is watching (in which nearly 50% of the films' contents and pixels are censored and removed).

Step 2 *Cinema 3-Step Solution* in Action     4:3-16:9 Aspect Ratio Movie Scene 2 visually cropped/censored by 50%

**Movie Scene 2**: A documentary about a beautiful constellation of stars that can only be seen a few days each
year.                     *Original Movie Aspect Ratio 4:3-16:9*

Step 2 *Cinema 3-Step Solution* in Action     4:3-16:9 Aspect Ratio Movie Scene 2 visually cropped/censored by 50%

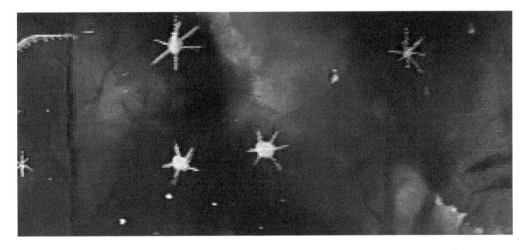

This movie scene has been cropped/visually censored to the cellphone-aspect ratios of 19:9-21:9. Nearly half of
the sky clouds are completely removed from the film. Nearly 1/2 of the constellation's stars are removed
from this film's scene. The constellation is now practically indecipherable and no a longer a constellation as
half of the stars have been removed from the film's scene. Nearly 50% of this movie's scene has been
cropped/visually censored and removed entirely from the film: this is a blatant violation of freedom,
freedom of speech, freedom of media consumption, and copyrights.

### *Section 3 Part 2*          *Step 2 of the Cinema 3-Step Solution*

Step 2 *Cinema 3-Step Solution* in Action      4:3-16:9 Aspect Ratio Movie Scene 3 visually cropped/censored by 50%

**Movie Scene 3**: A science fiction movie where the lead character shows the village where she grew up.
*Original Movie Aspect Ratio 4:3-16:9*

Step 2 *Cinema 3-Step Solution* in Action      4:3-16:9 Aspect Ratio Movie Scene 3 visually cropped/censored by 50%

This movie scene has been cropped/visually censored to the cellphone-aspect ratios of 19:9-21:9. None of the village's homes can be seen in their entirety after being visually censored and cropped. The grass scenery up river is completely removed from the film's scene as if it never existed. The scene is completely diminished from its original scene. The river's length is reduced in half. Nearly half of the scenery is removed from this scene. Nearly 50% of this movie's scene has been cropped/visually censored and removed entirely from the film: this is a blatant violation of freedom, freedom of speech, freedom of media consumption, and copyrights.

## Section 3 Part 2      Step 2 of the Cinema 3-Step Solution

Step 2 *Cinema 3-Step Solution* in Action     4:3-16:9 Aspect Ratio Movie Scene 4 visually cropped/censored by 50%

**Movie Scene 4**: A movie about a small-town community that holds its river as its vital source of energy and identity.     *Original Movie Aspect Ratio 4:3-16:9*

Step 2 *Cinema 3-Step Solution* in Action     4:3-16:9 Aspect Ratio Movie Scene 4 visually cropped/censored by 50%

This movie scene has been cropped/visually censored to the cellphone-aspect ratios of 19:9-21:9. Nearly half the river sw visually censored/cropped and removed from the film's scene. The scenes town is barely decipherable, as nearly 50% of the film's scenery in this scene has been removed. Nearly 50% of this movie's scene has been cropped/visually censored and removed entirely from the film: this is a blatant violation of freedom, freedom of speech, freedom of media consumption, and copyrights.

"If a museum's paintings were cropped/visually censored by 50%, there would be outrage, fines, and jail times to all parties and individuals involved. The cropping/visual censoring of cinematic movies by 50%, is no different a crime then cropping/visually censoring the paintings of a museum by 50%. At the bare minimum, movie streaming companies like Netflix, Hulu, Prime Video, Tubi, and YouTube Movie Channels should provide the consumer with the freedom, ability, and choice (Step 2 of the *Cinema 3-Step Solution*) for the consumer to choose to crop/visually censor "zoom to fill cellphone screen" the cinematic films that the consumer is watching."

Step 2 *Cinema 3-Step Solution* in Action     4:3-16:9 Aspect Ratio Movie Scene 5 visually cropped/censored by 50%

**Movie Scene 5**: A woman from the city retires from her work and changes her lifestyle to be in a beautiful forest full of greens and trees.     *Original Movie Aspect Ratio 4:3-16:9*

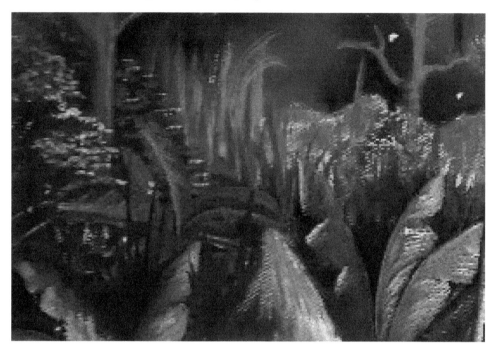

Step 2 *Cinema 3-Step Solution* in Action     4:3-16:9 Aspect Ratio Movie Scene 5 visually cropped/censored by 50%

This movie scene has been cropped/visually censored to the ultrawide cellphone aspect ratios of 19:9-21:9. Nearly half the plants and trees are removed from the film's scene. As nearly 50% of the film's contents have been removed, the scene is nearly indecipherable. Nearly 50% of this movie's scene has been cropped/visually censored and removed entirely from the film: this is a blatant violation of freedom, freedom of speech, freedom of media consumption, and copyrights.

"If a museum's paintings were cropped/visually censored by 50%, there would be outrage, fines, and jail times to all parties and individuals involved. The cropping/visual censoring of cinematic movies by 50%, is no different a crime then cropping/visually censoring the paintings of a museum by 50%. At the bare minimum, movie streaming companies like Netflix, Hulu, Prime Video, Tubi, and YouTube Movie Channels should provide the consumer with the freedom, ability, and choice (Step 2 of the *Cinema 3-Step Solution*) for the consumer to choose to crop/visually censor "zoom to fill cellphone screen" the cinematic films that the consumer is watching."

*Section 3 Part 2*                    *Step 2 of the Cinema 3-Step Solution*

Step 2 *Cinema 3-Step Solution* in Action        4:3-16:9 Aspect Ratio Movie Scene 6 visually cropped/censored by 50%

**Movie Scene 6:** A young man ponders the future while lying down and looking at the night sky.

*Original Movie Aspect Ratio 4:3-16:9*

Step 2 *Cinema 3-Step Solution* in Action        4:3-16:9 Aspect Ratio Movie Scene 6 visually cropped/censored by 50%

This movie scene has been cropped/visually censored to the cellphone-aspect ratios of 19:9-21:9. Half of the night sky's stars are censored, and half of the ground is censored. The ground is almost entirely removed from this scene. About half of the stars are removed from this scene. Nearly 50% of this movie's scene has been cropped/visually censored and removed entirely from the film: this is a blatant violation of freedom, freedom of speech, freedom of media consumption, and copyrights.

"The cropping/visual censoring of cinematic movies by 50%, is no different a crime then cropping/visually censoring the paintings of a museum by 50%. At the bare minimum, movie streaming companies like Netflix, Hulu, Prime Video, Tubi, and YouTube Movie Channels should provide the consumer with the freedom, ability, and choice (Step 2 of the *Cinema 3-Step Solution*) for the consumer to choose to crop/visually censor "zoom to fill cellphone screen" the cinematic films that the consumer is watching."

Step 2 *Cinema 3-Step Solution* in Action     4:3-16:9 Aspect Ratio Movie Scene 7 visually cropped/censored by 50%

**Movie Scene 7**: A nature program about a rare type of tree that exists in only certain parts of the world.

*Original Movie Aspect Ratio 4:3-16:9*

Step 2 *Cinema 3-Step Solution* in Action     4:3-16:9 Aspect Ratio Movie Scene 7 visually cropped/censored by 50%

This movie scene has been cropped/visually censored to the cellphone-aspect ratios of 19:9-21:9. Nearly half of the trees are removed from the scene. The roots and the very top branch branches are completely removed from the scene. The moon is completely removed from the scene. The beach trees are completely removed from the scene. Nearly 50% of this movie's scene has been cropped/visually censored and removed entirely from the film: this is a blatant violation of freedom, freedom of speech, freedom of media consumption, and copyrights.

"If a museum's paintings were cropped/visually censored by 50%, there would be outrage, fines, and jail times to all parties and individuals involved. The cropping/visual censoring of cinematic movies by 50%, is no different a crime then cropping/visually censoring the paintings of a museum by 50%. At the bare minimum, movie streaming companies like Netflix, Hulu, Prime Video, Tubi, and YouTube Movie Channels should provide the consumer with the freedom, ability, and choice (Step 2 of the *Cinema 3-Step Solution*) for the consumer to choose to crop/visually censor "zoom to fill cellphone screen" the cinematic films that the consumer is watching."

Step 2 *Cinema 3-Step Solution* in Action     4:3-16:9 Aspect Ratio Movie Scene 8 visually cropped/censored by 50%

**Movie Scene 8**: An animated movie of the life a bird that explores the lands, the stars, the forests, and the world.

*Original Movie Aspect Ratio 4:3-16:9*

Step 2 *Cinema 3-Step Solution* in Action     4:3-16:9 Aspect Ratio Movie Scene 8 visually cropped/censored by 50%

This movie scene has been cropped/visually censored to the cellphone-aspect ratios of 19:9-21:9. Half of the world is removed and the land and stars are barely visible. The explorable world that the bird has to experience and explore is reduced in size by nearly 50%. Nearly 50% of this movie's scene has been cropped/visually censored and removed entirely from the film: this is a blatant violation of freedom, freedom of speech, freedom of media consumption, and copyrights.

"If a museum's paintings were cropped/visually censored by 50%, there would be outrage, fines, and jail times to all parties and individuals involved. The cropping/visual censoring of cinematic movies by 50%, is no different a crime then cropping/visually censoring the paintings of a museum by 50%. At the bare minimum, movie streaming companies like Netflix, Hulu, Prime Video, Tubi, and YouTube Movie Channels should provide the consumer with the freedom, ability, and choice (Step 2 of the *Cinema 3-Step Solution*) for the consumer to choose to crop/visually censor "zoom to fill cellphone screen" the cinematic films that the consumer is watching."

*Section 3 Part 2*         *Step 2 of the Cinema 3-Step Solution*

Step 2 *Cinema 3-Step Solution* in Action      4:3-16:9 Aspect Ratio Movie Scene 9 visually cropped/censored by 50%

**Movie Scene 9**: A movie which shows the lifestyle of an old man who tells his life adventures next to the river.

*Original Movie Aspect Ratio 4:3-16:9*

Step 2 *Cinema 3-Step Solution* in Action      4:3-16:9 Aspect Ratio Movie Scene 9 visually cropped/censored by 50%

This movie scene has been cropped/visually censored to the cellphone-aspect ratios of 19:9-21:9. The scene is barely visible. The village is barely decipherable. Most of the trees' roots and branches are removed from the scene. The size of the river is reduced, and the large tree's roots and nearby sticks are completely removed from the scene. Nearly 50% of this movie's scene has been cropped/visually censored and removed entirely from the film: this is a blatant violation of freedom, freedom of speech, freedom of media consumption, and copyrights.

"If a museum's paintings were cropped/visually censored by 50%, there would be outrage, fines, and significant jail times to all parties and individuals involved. The cropping/visual censoring of cinematic movies by 50%, is no different a crime then cropping/visually censoring the paintings of a museum by 50%. At the bare minimum, movie streaming companies like Netflix, Hulu, Prime Video, Tubi, and YouTube Movie Channels should provide the consumer with the freedom, ability, and choice (Step 2 of the *Cinema 3-Step Solution*) for the consumer to choose to crop/visually censor "zoom to fill cellphone screen" the cinematic films that the consumer is watching."

# How Cellphones Cropped, Distorted, and Visually Censored Cinema: Let's Save Cinema Page 59
## *Section 3 Part 2*        *Step 2 of the Cinema 3-Step Solution*
### 4:3-16:9 aspect ratio films visually cropped/censored by nearly 50%)

Conclusion:

No matter the cinematic film, no matter the scene, the visual cropping/censorship of cinema removes nearly half of the films' original contents, pixels, and experiences. The removal of nearly half of "copyrighted" films' contents and pixels is a blatant violation of copyrights and a blatant violation of freedom, freedom of speech, and freedom of media consumption. The visual censorship and cropping of cinematic films initiated by movie streaming companies such as Netflix, Hulu, Prime Video, Tubi, and official Youtube Movie Channels denies the consumer freedom of media consumption, as the consumer is only able to watch about 50% of the film's original contents. The visual cropping/censorship of films is no different a crime than visually cropping/censoring paintings in museums by 50%. The removal of content is censorship. Museums do not crop and cut paintings by 50%, and if they did there would be serious legal ramifications, jail time, and fines to all parties and individuals involved. Why is it okay for movie streaming companies like Netflix, Prime Video, Hulu, Tubi, and official YouTube movie channels to visually crop/censor and remove nearly 50% of most films' contents and pixels? There is no difference between a copyrighted painting and a copyrighted cinematic film.

Step 2 of the *Cinema 3-Step Solution* offers the consumer the freedom, ability, and choice to consume cinematic films in a visually cropped/censored manner. In Step 2, consumers have the ability and choice to watch films cropped/visually censored to fill the size of their cellphone devices' screen with the "zoom to fill" feature.

Step 2 of the *Cinema 3-Step Solution* provides non-enjoyable, non-simulative, non-immersive, and significantly reduced cinematic experiences. Cinematic films both native or cropped/visually censored to the ultrawide 19:9-21:9 cellphone-aspect ratios, do not simulate the visual euphoria and do not simulate the visual immersion of cinema. The visual euphoria and visual immersion of cinema does not occur for cinematic films presented in the 19:9-21:9 aspect ratios, as the 19:9-21:9 aspect ratios provide and simulate about only 50% of the field of view our anatomical eyes experience sight and vision in real life. When we watch movies that are presented in the cellphone aspect ratios of 19:9-21:9 aspect ratios, visual euphoria and visual immersions do not occur as the mind can tell the difference between what is real and what is not real. The 19:9-21:9 aspect ratios do not simulate the aspect ratios (or field of views) our eyes experience field of vision (the standard sight of the human eyes sees in field of views somewhere between the 4:3-16:9 aspect ratios).

# Step 3 of

# The *Cinema 3-Step Solution*

## to End the Forced Visual Cropping/Censorship and Distortion of Cinema:

**Step 3:** If the consumer is watching a movie on a cellphone device, the consumer has the freedom, ability, and choice to click "distort to fit cellphone screen" (which distorts, morphs, junks, and composts a film's original size and contents by reducing the film's size, contents, and pixels by nearly 50% at the vertical length). Alternatively, the cellphone consumer can initiate *Step 1* of the *Cinema 3-Step Solution* or *Step 2* of the *Cinema 3-Step Solution.*

# Step 3 of

# The *Cinema 3-Step Solution*

Step 3 *Cinema 3-Step Solution* in Action   4:3-16:9 Aspect Ratio Movie Scene 1 visually distorted & junked by 50%

**Movie Scene 1**: A documentary about the moon which shows beautiful footage of the moon.

*Original Movie Aspect Ratio: 4:3-16:9*

Step 3 *Cinema 3-Step Solution* in Action     4:3-16:9 Aspect Ratio Movie Scene 1 visually distorted & junked by 50%

**Commentary for Step 3 is not needed, apart from this statement which will be repeated for each movie's scene:**

"This movie's scene has been distorted, junked, morphed, and composted to be nearly 50% less in size (the size of cellphone aspect ratios 19:9-21:9): this is a blatant violation and disregard of freedom, freedom of speech, freedom of media consumption, and copyrights.

If a museum's paintings were distorted, junked, morphed, and composted to be nearly 50% less in size at the vertical length, there would be outrage, fines, and jail times to all parties and individuals involved. The distortion, junking, and composting of cinematic films is no different a crime then distorting, junking, and composting paintings to be nearly 50% less in size. At the bare minimum, movie streaming companies like Netflix, Hulu, Prime Video, Tubi, and Official Youtube Movie channels should provide consumers with the freedom, ability, and choice (Step 3 of *the Cinema 3-Step Solution*) to choose to distort/junk/compost/morph "distort to fit cellphone screen" the cinematic films that they are watching."

*Section 3 Part 3* *Step 3 of the Cinema 3-Step Solution*

Step 3 *Cinema 3-Step Solution* in Action   4:3-16:9 Aspect Ratio Movie Scene 2 visually distorted & junked by 50%

**Movie Scene 2**: A documentary about a beautiful constellation of stars that can only be seen a few days each year. *Original Movie Aspect Ratio: 4:3-16:9*

Step 3 *Cinema 3-Step Solution* in Action     4:3-16:9 Aspect Ratio Movie Scene 2 visually distorted & junked by 50%

"This movie scene has been distorted/junked/composted/morphed to the cellphone-aspect ratios of 19:9-21:9. This movie's scene has been distorted, junked, morphed, and composted to be nearly 50% less in size (the size of cellphone- aspect ratios 19:9-21:9): this is a blatant violation and disregard of freedom, freedom of speech, freedom of media consumption, and copyrights. If a museum's paintings were distorted, junked, and composted to be nearly 50% less in size at the vertical length, there would be outrage, fines, and jail times to all parties and individuals involved. The distortion, junking, and composting of cinematic films is no different a crime then distorting, junking, morphing, and composting paintings to be nearly 50% less in size. At the bare minimum, movie streaming companies like Netflix, Hulu, Prime Video, Tubi, and Official Youtube Movie channels should provide consumers with the freedom, ability, and choice (Step 3 of *the Cinema 3-Step Solution*) to choose to distort/junk/compost "distort to fit cellphone screen" the cinematic films that they are watching."

*Section 3 Part 3*        *Step 3 of the Cinema 3-Step Solution*

Step 3 *Cinema 3-Step Solution* in Action   4:3-16:9 Aspect Ratio Movie Scene 3 visually distorted & junked by 50%

**Movie Scene 3**: A science fiction movie where the lead character shows the village where she grew up.

*Original Movie Aspect Ratio: 4:3-16:9*

Step 3 *Cinema 3-Step Solution* in Action      4:3-16:9 Aspect Ratio Movie Scene 3 visually distorted & junked by 50%

"This movie scene has been distorted/junked/composted/morphed to the cellphone-aspect ratios of 19:9-21:9. This movie's scene has been distorted, junked, morphed, and composted to be nearly 50% less in size (the size of cellphone- aspect ratios 19:9-21:9): this is a blatant violation and disregard of freedom, freedom of speech, freedom of media consumption, and copyrights. If a museum's paintings were distorted, junked, and composted to be nearly 50% less in size at the vertical length, there would be outrage, fines, and jail times to all parties and individuals involved. The distortion, junking, and composting of cinematic films is no different a crime then distorting, junking, and composting paintings to be nearly 50% less in size."

Step 3 *Cinema 3-Step Solution* in Action   4:3-16:9 Aspect Ratio Movie Scene 4 visually distorted & junked by 50%

**Movie Scene 4**: A movie about a small-town community that holds its river as its vital source of energy and identity.                    *Original Movie Aspect Ratio: 4:3-16:9*

Step 3 *Cinema 3-Step Solution* in Action     4:3-16:9 Aspect Ratio Movie Scene 4 visually distorted & junked by 50%

"This movie scene has been distorted/junked/composted/morphed to the cellphone aspect ratios of 19:9-21:9. This movie's scene has been distorted, junked, morphed, and composted to be nearly 50% less in size (the size of cellphone- aspect ratios 19:9-21:9): this is a blatant violation and disregard of freedom, freedom of speech, freedom of media consumption, and copyrights. If a museum's paintings were distorted, junked, and composted to be nearly 50% less in size at the vertical length, there would be outrage, fines, and jail times to all parties and individuals involved. The distortion, junking, and composting of cinematic films is no different a crime then distorting, junking, and composting paintings to be nearly 50% less in size. At the bare minimum, movie streaming companies like Netflix, Hulu, Prime Video, Tubi, and Official Youtube Movie channels should provide consumers with the freedom, ability, and choice (Step 3 of *the Cinema 3-Step Solution*) for to choose to distort/junk/compost "distort to fit cellphone screen" the cinematic films that they are watching."

Step 3 *Cinema 3-Step Solution* in Action   4:3-16:9 Aspect Ratio Movie Scene 5 visually distorted & junked by 50%

**Movie Scene 5**: A woman from the city retires from her work and changes her lifestyle to be in a beautiful forest full of greens and trees.           *Original Movie Aspect Ratio: 4:3-16:9*

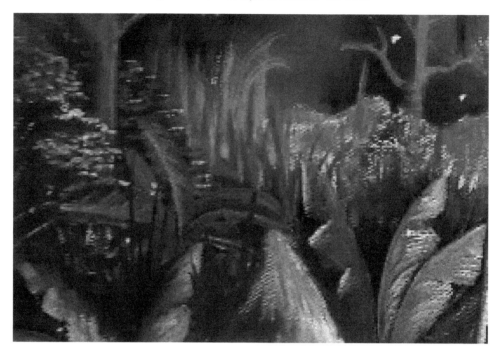

Step 3 *Cinema 3-Step Solution* in Action     4:3-16:9 Aspect Ratio Movie Scene 5 visually distorted & junked by 50%

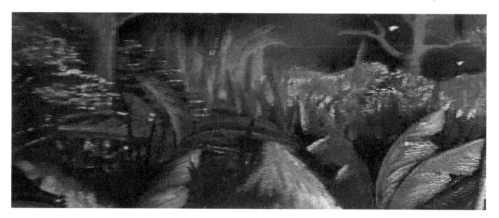

"This movie scene has been distorted/junked/composted/morphed to the cellphone-aspect ratios of 19:9-21:9. This movie's scene has been distorted, junked, morphed, and composted to be nearly 50% less in size (the size of cellphone-aspect ratios 19:9-21:9): this is a blatant violation and disregard of freedom, freedom of speech, freedom of media consumption, and copyrights. If a museum's paintings were distorted, junked, and composted to be nearly 50% less in size at the vertical length, there would be outrage, fines, and jail times to all parties and individuals involved. The distortion, junking, and composting of cinematic films is no different a crime then distorting, junking, and composting paintings to be nearly 50% less in size. At the bare minimum, movie streaming companies like Netflix, Hulu, Prime Video, Tubi, and Official Youtube Movie channels should provide consumers with the freedom, ability, and choice (Step 3 of *the Cinema 3-Step Solution*) to choose to distort/junk/compost "distort to fit cellphone screen" the cinematic films that they are watching."

Step 3 *Cinema 3-Step Solution* in Action    4:3-16:9 Aspect Ratio Movie Scene 6 visually distorted & junked by 50%

**Movie Scene 6**: A young man ponders the future while lying down and looking at the night sky.

*Original Movie Aspect Ratio: 4:3-16:9*

Step 3 *Cinema 3-Step Solution* in Action      4:3-16:9 Aspect Ratio Movie Scene 6 visually distorted & junked by 50%

"This movie's scene has been distorted, junked, morphed, and composted to be nearly 50% less in size (the size of cellphone- aspect ratios 19:9-21:9): this is a blatant violation and disregard of freedom, freedom of speech, freedom of media consumption, and copyrights. If a museum's paintings were distorted, junked, morphed, and composted to be nearly 50% less in size at the vertical length, there would be outrage, fines, and jail times to all parties and individuals involved. The distortion, junking, and composting of cinematic films is no different a crime then distorting, junking, and composting paintings to be nearly 50% less in size. At the bare minimum, movie streaming companies like Netflix, Hulu, Prime Video, Tubi, and Official Youtube Movie channels should provide consumers with the freedom, ability, and choice (Step 3 of *the Cinema 3-Step Solution*) to choose to distort/junk/compost/morph "distort to fit cellphone screen" the cinematic films that they are watching."

***Section 3 Part 3***          ***Step 3 of the Cinema 3-Step Solution***

Step 3 *Cinema 3-Step Solution* in Action    4:3-16:9 Aspect Ratio Movie Scene 7 visually distorted & junked by 50%

**Movie Scene 7**: A nature program about a rare type of tree that exists in only certain parts of the world.

*Original Movie Aspect Ratio: 4:3-16:9*

Step 3 *Cinema 3-Step Solution* in Action      4:3-16:9 Aspect Ratio Movie Scene 7 visually distorted & junked by 50%

    "This movie scene has been distorted/junked/composted/morphed to the cellphone-aspect ratios of 19:9-21:9. This movie's scene has been distorted, junked, morphed, and composted to be nearly 50% less in size (the size of cellphone-aspect ratios 19:9-21:9): this is a blatant violation and disregard of freedom, freedom of speech, freedom of media consumption, and copyrights. If a museum's paintings were distorted, junked, and composted to be nearly 50% less in size at the vertical length, there would be outrage, fines, and jail times to all parties and individuals involved. The distortion, junking, and composting of cinematic films is no different a crime then distorting, junking, and composting paintings to be nearly 50% less in size. At the bare minimum, movie streaming companies like Netflix, Hulu, Prime Video, Tubi, and Official Youtube Movie channels should provide consumers with the freedom, ability, and choice (Step 3 of *the Cinema 3-Step Solution*) to choose to distort/junk/compost "distort to fit cellphone screen" the cinematic films that they are watching."

Step 3 *Cinema 3-Step Solution* in Action    4:3-16:9 Aspect Ratio Movie Scene 8 visually distorted & junked by 50%

**Movie Scene 8**: an animated movie of the life a bird that explores the lands, the stars, the forests, and the world.      *Original Movie Aspect Ratio: 4:3-16:9*

Step 3 *Cinema 3-Step Solution* in Action      4:3-16:9 Aspect Ratio Movie Scene 8 visually distorted & junked by 50%

"This movie scene has been distorted/junked/composted/morphed to the cellphone-aspect ratios of 19:9-21:9. This movie's scene has been distorted, junked, morphed, and composted to be nearly 50% less in size (the size of cellphone-aspect ratios 19:9-21:9): this is a blatant violation and disregard of freedom, freedom of speech, freedom of media consumption, and copyrights. If a museum's paintings were distorted, junked, and composted to be nearly 50% less in size at the vertical length, there would be outrage, fines, and jail times to all parties and individuals involved. The distortion, junking, and composting of cinematic films is no different a crime then distorting, junking, and composting paintings to be nearly 50% less in size. At the bare minimum, movie streaming companies like Netflix, Hulu, Prime Video, Tubi, and Official Youtube Movie channels should provide consumers with the freedom, ability, and choice (Step 3 of *the Cinema 3-Step Solution*) to choose to distort/junk/compost/morph "distort to fit cellphone screen" the cinematic films that they are watching."

Step 3 *Cinema 3-Step Solution* in Action   4:3-16:9 Aspect Ratio Movie Scene 9 visually distorted & junked by 50%

**Movie Scene 9**: A movie which shows the lifestyle of an old man who tells his life adventures next to the river.          *Original Movie Aspect Ratio: 4:3-16:9*

Step 3 *Cinema 3-Step Solution* in Action     4:3-16:9 Aspect Ratio Movie Scene 9 visually distorted & junked by 50%

"This movie scene has been distorted/junked/composted to the cellphone-aspect ratios of 19:9-21:9.

This movie's scene has been distorted, junked, morphed, and composted to be nearly 50% less in size (the size of cellphone- aspect ratios 19:9-21:9): this is a blatant violation and disregard of freedom, freedom of speech, freedom of media consumption, and copyrights. If a museum's paintings were distorted, junked, morphed, and composted to be nearly 50% less in size at the vertical length, there would be outrage, fines, and jail times to all parties and individuals involved. The distortion, junking, and composting of cinematic films is no different a crime then distorting, junking, and composting paintings to be nearly 50% less in size. At the bare minimum, movie streaming companies like Netflix, Hulu, Prime Video, Tubi, and Official Youtube Movie channels should provide consumers with the freedom, ability, and choice (Step 3 of *the Cinema 3-Step Solution*) to choose to distort/junk/compost/morph "distort to fit cellphone screen" the cinematic films that they are watching."

How Cellphones Cropped, Distorted, and Visually Censored Cinema: Let's Save Cinema Page 71
*Section 3 Part 3*              *Step 3 of the Cinema 3-Step Solution*
Step 3 *Cinema 3-Step Solution* in Action   4:3-16:9 Aspect Ratio Movies visually distorted & junked by 50%

Conclusion:

No matter the cinematic film, no matter the scene, the visual distortion/junking/morphing/composting of cinema to the ultrawide cellphone-aspect ratios of 19:9-21:9, makes the scene non-simulative, non-immersive, non-realistic, non-enjoyable, and provides a very limited field of view. Cinematic films when cropped/visually censored or distorted/junked/composted to the 19:9-21:9 aspect ratios provide non-simulative and non-enjoyable experiences.

The 19:9-21:9 aspect ratios provide non-immersive, non-simulative, non-entertaining, and non-enjoyable experiences because the standard human vision of the human eyes experiences sight in the 4:3-16:9 aspect ratios (or field of views) and not in the cellphone-aspect ratios (19:9-21:9 aspect ratios). The 19:9-21:9 aspect ratios only simulate about 50% of the standard sight and field of view of standard vision, and as a result, the mind is not immersed and not simulated with the cinematic film presented. The results and effects of cinematic films either cropped/visually censored, distorted/junked/composted, or filmed natively in 19:9-21:9 aspect ratios are contraindicative to the very definition of the word "cinema". The ultrawide cellphone- aspect ratios of 19:9-21:9 fail to offer any benefits or advantages to the cinematic experience, and instead only offer cons, disadvantages, and negative effects.

The distortion of cinematic films is also a blatant violation of copyrights as the physical structure of a cinematic film is entirely changed, distorted, morphed, junked, and composted at the contents & pixel level by nearly 50% to be nearly 50% less in size at the vertical length. The distortion, junking, morphing, and composting of "copyrighted" cinematic films' contents & pixels to be nearly 50% less in size at the vertical length is a blatant violation of copyrights and a blatant violation of freedom, freedom of speech, and freedom of media consumption.

The visual distortion, morphing, junking, and composting of cinematic films initiated by movie streaming companies such as Netflix, Hulu, Prime Video, Tubi, and official Youtube Movie Channels denies the consumer freedom & and freedom of media consumption, as the consumer is only able to watch films after the film has been distorted, junked, and composted to be 50% less in size. The distortion, junking, and composting of films is no different a crime than collecting paintings in a museum and placing them in a builder's shed and having them distorted, junked, morphed, and composted to be nearly 50% less in size at the vertical length. The distortion, junking, morphing, and composting of films is a blatant violation of copyrights, freedom, freedom of speech, and denies the consumer freedom of media consumption.

Museums do not distort, junk, and compost paintings, and if they did there would be serious legal repercussions, jail time, and fines to all parties and individuals involved. Why is it okay for movie streaming companies like Netflix, Prime Video, Hulu, Tubi, and official Youtube movie channels to distort, morph, junk, and compost most films contents and pixels to be nearly 50% percent less in size at the vertical length size? There is no difference between a copyrighted painting and a copyrighted cinematic film.

Step 3 of the *Cinema 3-Step Solution* provides consumers with the freedom, ability, and choice to consume cinematic movies in a visually distorted manner. In Step 3, the consumer has the freedom, ability, and choice to watch films distorted to the size of their cellphone devices' screens with the "distort to fit screen" feature.

**How Cellphones Cropped, Distorted, and Visually Censored Cinema: Let's Save Cinema** Page 72
*Section 3 Part 3*          *Step 3 of the Cinema 3-Step Solution*
Step 3 *Cinema 3-Step Solution* in Action   4:3-16:9 Aspect Ratio Movies visually distorted & junked by 50%

Conclusion Continued:

Step 3 like Step 2 provides a non-simulative, non-immersive, and non-enjoyable cinematic experience. Step 3 like Step 2 of the *Cinema 3-Step Solution*, offers limited experiences which do not simulate the standard sight, vision, and field of view of the human eyes. Films distorted/junked/composted to the 19:9-21:9 cellphone-aspect ratios only simulate about 50% of the standard field of view and sight of the human eyes. In the case of films presented in the 19:9-21:9 aspect ratios, the human brain is not tricked into being entertained, and as a result, a non-enjoyable cinematic experience occurs. Cinematic films distorted to the cellphone-aspect ratios of 19:9-21:9 do not activate the phenomenon of visual euphoria (the visual euphoria of cinema occurs when we watch films that are presented in the aspect ratios (or field of views) of 4:3-16:9 which simulate how our eyes see and experience sight and field of views in real life).

In addition, cinematic films cropped/visually censored, distorted/junked, or filmed natively in the 19:9-21:9 aspect ratios are contraindicative to the very definition of the word "cinema" at the scientific anatomical level of the human eyes. The visual euphoria, visual simulation, and visual immersion of cinema does not occur for movies presented in the 19:9-21:9 aspect ratios, as they provide and simulate about only 50% of the field of view our anatomical eyes experience sight and field of vision in real life. When we watch movies that are presented in the aspect ratios of 19:9-21:9, visual euphorias and visual immersions do not occur, as the mind can tell the difference between what is real and what is not real. Step 3 in some ways is worse than Step 2, as the distortion of films changes the entire structure of films as the cinematic movies are distorted, junked, and composted at the structural pixel level to be nearly 50% less in size at the vertical length. The distortion, morphing, junking, and composting of films is a blatant violation of freedom and the principles of copyright laws, as the product is changed from one product to an entirely new product that has been damaged, junked, and composted at the structural level to be 50% less in size.

The *Cinema-3 Step Solution* provides a legal cure for movie streaming companies and official Youtube movie channels to provide and comply with freedom, freedom of speech, freedom of media consumption, and copyrights. By presenting all cinematic films across all applications and all devices in their original contents and original aspect ratios (Step 1), freedom of media consumption and the protection of copyrighted films occurs. If consumers want to crop/visually censor their cinematic film on their cellphone device (Step 2), consumers have the freedom, ability, and choice to "zoom to fill" their cinematic film to their cellphone device. If consumers want to distort/junk/compost a cinematic film to be nearly 50% less in size on their cellphone device (Step 3), consumers have the freedom, ability, and choice to "distort to fit" their cinematic film to their cellphone devices' screen aspect ratios. The fact of the matter is that the technology to apply the *Cinema 3-Step Solution* has already been in existence and installed on bargain DVD players and DVD player applications for over a decade. There is no reason for movie streaming companies like Netflix, Hulu, Prime Video, Tubi, and Official Youtube movie channels to not include the *Cinema 3-Step Solution*. If small teams of developers can honor freedom of speech, freedom of media consumption, and copyrights when they make DVD players and DVD player applications, there is no excuse for massive streaming companies to violate the copyrights of cinematic films and deny the global consumer freedom of media consumption by forcing consumers to access films only after they have cropped/visually censored films by nearly 50%, or distorted/junked/composted films by nearly 50%.

# Step 1, Step 2, and Step 3 of

# The *Cinema 3-Step Solution*

# *In Action as a Complete Solution*

## to End the Forced Visual Cropping/Censorship and Distortion of Cinema:

**Step 1:** Provide movies in their original contents & original aspect ratios without visually cropping/censoring or distorting/morphing/junking/composting the films' contents and pixels.

*Note:* When a modern cellphone is being used horizontally, it can display films made in every type of cinematic aspect ratio ever made (whether the film is the 4:3, 16:9, 18:9, 19.5, or 21:9 aspect ratio) without the film being cropped/censored or distorted in any way as the part of the cellphone screen not being used displays black bars/black spaces/black curtains.

**Step 2:** If the consumer is watching a movie on a cellphone device, the consumer has the freedom, ability, and choice to click "zoom to fill cellphone screen" (which visually crops/censors the film by nearly 50% percent). Alternatively, the cellphone consumer can return to *Step 1* of the *Cinema 3-Step Solution* and watch the movie without the movie being visually cropped/censored.

**Step 3:** If the consumer is watching a movie on a cellphone device, the consumer has the freedom, ability, and choice to click "distort to fit cellphone screen" (which distorts, morphs, junks, and composts a film's original size and contents by reducing the film's size, contents, and pixels by nearly 50% at the vertical length). Alternatively, the cellphone consumer can initiate *Step 1* of the *Cinema 3-Step Solution* or *Step 2* of the *Cinema 3-Step Solution.*

### Freedom of Media Consumption = The *Cinema 3-Step Solution*

The *Cinema 3-Step Solution* provides the consumer the ability, freedom, and choice to watch a film in its original contents & original aspect ratio (Step 1),

to watch a film visually cropped/censored (Step 2),

and to watch a film distorted/junked/composted/morphed (Step 3).

# Step 1, Step 2, and Step 3

# of

# The *Cinema 3-Step Solution*

# *In Action as a Complete Solution*

to End the Forced Visual Cropping/Censorship and Distortion of Cinema:

Step 1 *Cinema 3-Step Solution* in Action   4:3-16:9 Original Aspect Ratio Movie Scene 1

Step 2 *Cinema 3-Step Solution* in Action     4:3-16:9 Aspect Ratio Movie Scene 1 visually cropped/censored by 50%

Step 3 *Cinema 3-Step Solution* in Action     4:3-16:9 Aspect Ratio Movie Scene 1 visually distorted & junked by 50%

**Section 3**             **Complete Comparative Conclusions of the *Cinema 3-Step Solution***

Step 1 *Cinema 3-Step Solution* in Action   4:3-16:9 Original Aspect Ratio Movie Scene 2

Step 2 *Cinema 3-Step Solution* in Action     4:3-16:9 Aspect Ratio Movie Scene 2 visually cropped/censored by 50%

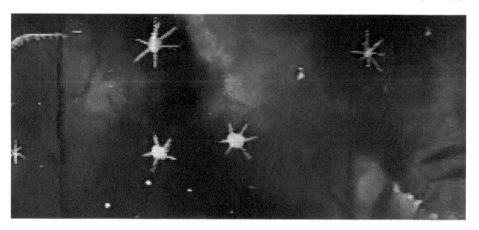

Step 3 *Cinema 3-Step Solution* in Action     4:3-16:9 Aspect Ratio Movie Scene 2 visually distorted & junked by 50%

Step 1 *Cinema 3-Step Solution* in Action    4:3-16:9 Original Aspect Ratio Movie Scene 3

Step 2 *Cinema 3-Step Solution* in Action     4:3-16:9 Aspect Ratio Movie Scene 3 visually cropped/censored by 50%

Step 3 *Cinema 3-Step Solution* in Action     4:3-16:9 Aspect Ratio Movie Scene 3 visually distorted & junked by 50%

Step 1 *Cinema 3-Step Solution* in Action   4:3-16:9 Original Aspect Ratio Movie Scene 4

Step 2 *Cinema 3-Step Solution* in Action      4:3-16:9 Aspect Ratio Movie Scene 4 visually cropped/censored by 50%

Step 3 *Cinema 3-Step Solution* in Action      4:3-16:9 Aspect Ratio Movie Scene 4 visually distorted & junked by 50%

Step 1 *Cinema 3-Step Solution* in Action   4:3-16:9 Original Aspect Ratio Movie Scene 5

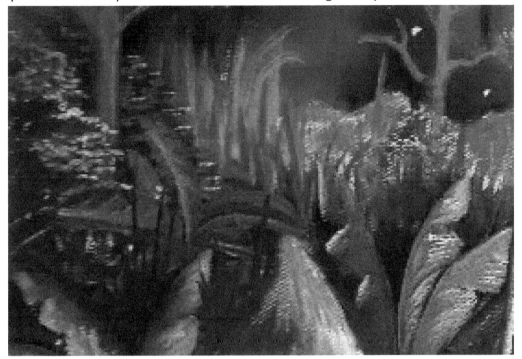

Step 2 *Cinema 3-Step Solution* in Action      4:3-16:9 Aspect Ratio Movie Scene 5 visually cropped/censored by 50%

Step 3 *Cinema 3-Step Solution* in Action      4:3-16:9 Aspect Ratio Movie Scene 5 visually distorted & junked by 50%

**Section 3**          **Complete Comparative Conclusions of the *Cinema 3-Step Solution***

Step 1 *Cinema 3-Step Solution* in Action    4:3-16:9 Original Aspect Ratio Movie Scene 6

Step 2 *Cinema 3-Step Solution* in Action      4:3-16:9 Aspect Ratio Movie Scene 6 visually cropped/censored by 50%

Step 3 *Cinema 3-Step Solution* in Action      4:3-16:9 Aspect Ratio Movie Scene 6 visually distorted & junked by 50%

**Section 3          Complete Comparative Conclusions of the *Cinema 3-Step Solution***

Step 1 *Cinema 3-Step Solution* in Action   4:3-16:9 Original Aspect Ratio Movie Scene 7

Step 2 *Cinema 3-Step Solution* in Action      4:3-16:9 Aspect Ratio Movie Scene 7 visually cropped/censored by 50%

Step 3 *Cinema 3-Step Solution* in Action      4:3-16:9 Aspect Ratio Movie Scene 7 visually distorted & junked by 50%

Step 1 *Cinema 3-Step Solution* in Action   4:3-16:9 Original Aspect Ratio Movie Scene 8

Step 2 *Cinema 3-Step Solution* in Action     4:3-16:9 Aspect Ratio Movie Scene 8 visually cropped/censored by 50%

Step 3 *Cinema 3-Step Solution* in Action     4:3-16:9 Aspect Ratio Movie Scene 8 visually distorted & junked by 50%

**Section 3         Complete Comparative Conclusions of the *Cinema 3-Step Solution***

Step 1 *Cinema 3-Step Solution* in Action   4:3-16:9 Original Aspect Ratio Movie Scene 9

Step 2 *Cinema 3-Step Solution* in Action     4:3-16:9 Aspect Ratio Movie Scene 9 visually cropped/censored by 50%

Step 3 *Cinema 3-Step Solution* in Action     4:3-16:9 Aspect Ratio Movie Scene 9 visually distorted & junked by 50%

# End Of Section 3.

Use this page to take notes on Section 3.

## Section 4 Part 1: The advantages and disadvantages of the various cinematic aspect ratios

*There are more benefits to cinematic films presented in the 4:3-16:9 aspect ratios then the number of stars able to be seen on a clear night's vision.*

# The Benefits and Advantages of Cinematic Films in the 4:3-16:9 Aspect Ratios

**The Benefits and Advantages of Cinematic Films presented in the 4:3-16:9 aspect ratios**

1. **Visual Immersion:** The 4:3-16:9 Aspect Ratios provide excellent, exciting, and brilliant life-like immersions into cinematic films. 4:3-16:9 aspect ratios cause you to feel immersed within the films.

2. **Visual Simulation:** The 4:3-16:9 Aspect Ratios perfectly simulate the visual experiences of films. The 4:3-16:9 Aspect Ratios simulate films perfectly as they simulate the standard sight & field of view of the human eyes.

3. **Simulates the Standard Sight of the Human Eyes:** The 4:3-16:9 Aspect Ratios simulate the way we see and experience field of vision in life, as we experience sight between the 4:3-16:9 aspect ratios (this causes visual euphoria).

4. **Visual Euphoria:** The 4:3-16:9 Aspect Ratios simulate the standard field of visions and fields of view of the human eyes (4:3-16:9 aspect ratios) which causes visually euphoric experiences.

5. **Enjoyable Experiences:** The 4:3-16:9 Aspect Ratios cause excellent visual immersions, simulations, and visually euphoric experiences which creates great and enjoyable cinematic experiences.

6. **Escapes & Entering Other Worlds:** The 4:3-16:9 Aspect Ratios provide excellent visual immersions and simulations of cinematic films by simulating the aspect ratios of standard Human sight (4:3-16:9) which causes the phenomenon of feeling like you have escaped this world and entered the worlds of the cinematic movies that you are consuming.

7. **Realistic Field of Views:** The 4:3-16:9 Aspect Ratios provide realistic field of views which simulate the standard human sight's field of view which is somewhere between the 4:3-16:9 aspect ratios (which makes films easy to focus on).

8. **Easy to Focus on**: The 4:3-16:9 aspect ratios are very easy for both eyes to focus on the whole screen at once.

There are no benefits to films presented in the cellphone-aspect ratios of 19:9-21:9. Furthermore, there are no benefits to films either natively made, visually cropped/censored, or distorted/junked/composted to the cellphone-aspect ratios of 19:9-21:9. There are only disadvantages and contraindications of films presented in the aspect ratios of 19:9-21:9.

## The disadvantages and Contraindications of Cinematic Films in the 19:9-21:9 Aspect Ratios

**1. The 19:9-21:9 Aspect Ratios <u>Do Not</u> Cause Visual Immersion:** The 19:9-21:9 Aspect Ratios <u>do not</u> provide immersions into cinematic films. The scientific anatomical field of view of standard human sight falls in between the 4:3-16:9 aspect ratios. Cinematic films presented in the cellphone-aspect ratios <u>do not</u> cause you to feel immersed within the films that you watch, as 19:9-21:9 aspect ratio films <u>do not</u> simulate the standard sight, field of view, and vision of the human eyes (The human eyes experience sight, field of views, and vision somewhere between the 4:3-16:9 Aspect Ratios).

**2. The 19:9-21:9 Aspect Ratios <u>Do Not</u> Cause Visual Simulation:** The 19:9-21:9 Aspect Ratios do not simulate films' visual experiences. Cinematic films presented in the 19:9-21:9 Aspect Ratios <u>do not</u> simulate films as they <u>do not</u> simulate the standard sight, field of view, and vision of the human eyes.

**3. The 19:9-21:9 Aspect Ratios <u>Do Not</u> Simulate the Standard Sight of the Human Eyes:** Cinematic Films presented in the 19:9-21:9 Aspect Ratios <u>do not</u> simulate the way we see and experience vision in real life. As we experience sight somewhere between the 4:3-16:9 aspect ratios, cinematic films either native, visually cropped/censored, or distorted/junked/composted <u>do not</u> cause visually euphoric experiences.

**4. The 19:9-21:9 Aspect Ratios <u>Do Not</u> Cause Visual Euphoria:** The phenomenon of the mind experiencing visually euphoric experiences from cinematic films <u>does not</u> occur with films presented in the 19:9-21:9 Aspect Ratios, for the 19:9-21:9 aspect ratios <u>do not</u> simulate the standard field of visions and fields of view of the human eyes (4:3-16:9 aspect ratios). Cinematic films presented in 19:9-21:9 aspect ratios <u>do not</u> cause visual euphoric experiences.

**5. The 19:9-21:9 Aspect Ratios <u>Do Not</u> Cause Enjoyable Experiences:** The 19:9-21:9 Aspect Ratios <u>do not</u> cause visual immersions, they <u>do not</u> cause visual simulations, and <u>they do</u> not cause visual euphorias which creates an overall non-enjoyable, frustrating, and difficult cinematic experience.

**6. The 19:9-21:9 Aspect Ratios <u>Do Not</u> Cause Escapes Into Other Worlds:** The 19:9-21:9 Aspect Ratios <u>do not</u> provide visual immersions and they <u>do not</u> provide visual simulations of cinematic films, for they <u>do not</u> simulate the aspect ratios of standard human sight (4:3-16:9). Cinematic films presented in the aspect ratios of 19:9-21:9 <u>do not</u> cause the phenomenon of feeling like you have escaped this world and entered the worlds of the cinematic movie you are consuming. At the scientific anatomic level of the human eyes, the 19:9-21:9 aspect ratios <u>do not</u> cause escapes into other worlds, and they <u>do not</u> make you feel like you are entering the worlds of the cinematic movies you are consuming, as the 19:9-21:9 aspect ratios provide very limited and unrealistic field of views.

**7. The 19:9-21:9 Aspect Ratios _Do Not_ Provide Realistic Field of Views:** The 19:9-21:9 Aspect Ratios <u>do not</u> provide realistic field of views, as they <u>do not</u> simulate the standard human sight's field of view which is somewhere between the 4:3-16:9 aspect ratios. The 19:9-21:9 aspect ratios only simulate half of the field of view of the standard sight, vision, and field of views of the human eyes, and as result, provides a visually difficult cinematic experience.

**8. The 19:9-21:9 Aspect Ratios <u>Are Not</u> Easy to Focus on**: The 19:9-21:9 Aspect ratios are difficult to focus on as they simulate only 50% of the standard field of view, vision, and sight of the human eyes. Cinematic films presented in the 19:9-21:9 aspect ratios are difficult to focus on, as they <u>do not</u> fall within the standard aspect ratios (or fields of view) of the human eyes (the human eyes see between the 4:3-16:9 aspect ratios). It is very difficult for the human eyes to focus on the entire screen at once on 19:9-21:9 aspect ratio films, as the films are unnaturally horizontal. In contrast, the 4:3-16:9 aspect ratios are very easy for both eyes to focus on the whole screen at once, as the 4:3-16:9 aspect ratios simulate the standard sight, vision, and field of view of the human eyes.

# End of Section 4.

Use this page to take notes on Section 4.

# Section 5: Let's Save and Protect Cinema On all Devices and Applications By Applying the *Cinema 3-Step Solution*

Section 5: I created Section 5 to serve as a basic starter guide for Hollywood, Bollywood, South Indian Cinematic Companies, Official YouTube Movie Channels, and Movie Streaming Companies to honor and comply with freedom, freedom of speech, freedom of media consumption, and the copyrights of cinematic films across all devices and platforms. Section 5 includes a simple guide to provide Movie Streaming Companies a comprehensive guide to begin the process of saving, restoring, and protecting the contents & copyrights of cinematic movies across all devices, applications, and platforms. Following the startup guide on this page, I will display the *Cinema 3-Step Solution* in practice as the solution is applied on Cellphones, Tablets, Laptops, Desktops, and Televisions. Section 5 provides substantial examples of the Cinema 3-Step Solution applied across all devices, so that Hollywood, Bollywood, South Indian Cinematic Companies, and Movie Streaming Companies like Netflix, Hulu, Prime Video, Tubi, and official Youtube Movie Channels (I.E Shemaroo, Goldmines, Ultra Movie Parlor) can fully understand, visualize, and apply the *Cinema 3-Step Solution*.

## Guide to Save, Restore, and Protect Cinematic Films

**Task 1:** Apply the *Cinema 3-Step Solution*. The *Cinema 3-Step Solution* allows the consumer the ability, freedom, and choice to watch a film in its original contents and original aspect ratio (Step 1), to watch a film visually cropped/censored (Step 2) "Zoom to Fill Cellphone Screen", and to watch a film distorted/junked/composted "Distort to Fit Cellphone Screen" (Step 3).

**Task 2:** The *Cinema 3-Step Solution* is already installed on bargain DVD players and DVD playing applications. Discount DVD players and DVD Player Applications were created by small teams of individuals, and they honor and comply with freedom, freedom of speech, freedom of media consumption, and the copyrights of cinematic films. While applying the *Cinema 3-Step Solution*, it would be very helpful to consult the makers of DVD players and DVD Player Applications. If any questions arise while installing the *Cinema 3-Step Solution*, small teams of developers will be able to answer any questions. Bargain DVD players and DVD Player applications have applied the principles of the *Cinema 3-Step Solution*, as they have honored and complied with freedom, freedom of speech, freedom of media consumption, and the copyrights of cinematic films for well over a decade. There is no excuse for movie streaming companies like Netflix, Hulu, Prime Video, Tubi, and official Youtube movie channels to continue to deny the consumer freedom of media consumption by cropping/visually censoring films by nearly 50%. There is no excuse for movie streaming companies like Netflix, Hulu, Prime Video, Tubi, and official YouTube movie channels to continue to deny the consumer freedom & freedom of media consumption by distorting, junking, and composting the contents of cinematic movies by nearly 50% less in size at the vertical length. Honor and comply with freedom and freedom of speech. Honor freedom of media consumption and honor and comply with the protection copyrights of cinematic films, just as the developers of bargain DVD Players and DVD Player Applications have.

**Task 3:** Contact the inspirational legends behind the idea for the Cinema 3-Step Solution. I studied multiple DVD players and DVD player application to create a solution to save cinema on movie streaming platforms, applications, and devices. I thank the makers of the DVD Players and DVD Player Applications for creating the foundational inspirational source material behind the *Cinema 3-Step Solution* and for honoring and complying with freedom, freedom of speech, freedom of media consumption, and the copyrights of cinematic movies.

# Section 5: Let's Save and Protect Cinema On all Devices and Applications By Applying the *Cinema 3-Step Solution*

**Task 4:** Contact local, national, and worldwide media agencies and establish a certification for companies that honor and comply with freedom, freedom of speech, freedom of media consumption, and the copyrights of cinematic films that apply the principles of the *Cinema 3-Step Solution.*

**Task 5:** Once the movie streaming platform receives a certification for providing consumers the freedom, choice, and ability to consume and enjoy cinematic films in their original contents & original aspect ratios, the respective movie streaming platforms can wear the certification with honor with pride. Movie streaming platforms, Hollywood, South Indian Cinema, Bollywood, and Official YouTube Movie Channels must take a few simple, but crucial 3 steps (The *Cinema 3-Step Solution*) to save, restore, and protect cinema. In this book, I have been very critical towards movie streaming companies such as Netflix, Hulu, Prime Video, Tubi, and Official Youtube Movie channels (Shemaroo, Goldmines, Youtube Movies etc.) but that criticism stems from focusing on all my amazing memories and cinematic experiences that I enjoyed from using the services of movie streaming companies until the year 2016. Through this project and the *Cinema 3-Step Solution*, I applied my efforts to raise awareness and create a solution, so that the world and the current & future generations could enjoy cinematic films in their original contents and original aspect ratios. I think we can all agree that it should be a basic right of humanity, a basic right of freedom & freedom of speech, a basic right of copyright protection, and a basic right of freedom of media consumption that the global consumer and global citizen should be able to consume and enjoy cinematic films in their original contents & original aspect ratios without the films being visually cropped/censored by nearly 50% or visually distorted/junked/composted by nearly 50% in size at the vertical length. By studying bargain DVD Players and DVD Player applications, I was able to create the wordings for a solution (The *Cinema 3-Step Solution*) to uniformly and easily provide the consumer with the freedom, ability, and choice to consume cinematic films in their original aspect ratios, contents, and pixels (Step 1), visually cropped/censored "zoom to fill cellphone screen" (Step 2), or visually distorted/junked/composted "distort to fit cellphone screen" (Step 3).

**Task 6:** Be proud and know that you took a few, but very crucial steps to save, restore, and protect the contents & copyrights of cinematic movies for both the current generation and future generations. Be proud that you will have paved the way for the current generation and future generations to enjoy cinematic movies and experiences in their original contents & original aspect ratios with freedom & freedom of media consumption.

Right up until the halfway mark of working on this project, I wrote this book primarily to raise awareness. The solution for this book's project originated by chance after I purchased a bulk shipment of Bollywood and South Indian Cinematic DVDs. As I tried out the DVDs across various consoles, DVD Players, and DVD Player applications, I discovered the solution for this book, The *Cinema 3-Step Solution*. The day that I realized that not only is there a solution to save, restore, and protect cinema, but that the solution already exists on bargain DVD players and DVD player applications, I knew that this book could be a reality.

**The next few pages include a visualization of the *Cinema 3-Step Solution* installed on all common Devices.**

## Section 5:
Let's Save and Protect Cinema On all Devices and Applications
By Applying the *Cinema 3-Step Solution*
**(Before)**
**The Cropping, Distortion, and Visual Censorship of Cinema on Cellphones Initiated by Movie Streaming Companies such as Netflix, Prime Video, Tubi, Hulu, and Official YouTube Movie Channels...**

At the time of writing this page,
Movie Streaming Companies like Netflix, Hulu, Prime Video, Tubi, and official YouTube Movie Channels like Shemaroo, YouTube Movies, Ultra Movie Parlour, and Goldmines force the consumers to watch the majority of all films ever created either cropped/visually censored by 50% on cellphones (and all devices) or distorted, morphed, junked, and composted by 50% to be 50% less in size vertically.

Movie streaming companies do not provide you with the ability, freedom, and choice to consume and enjoy cinematic movies on cellphones (and all devices) in their original contents & original aspect ratios.

**These are blatant violations of freedom, freedom of media consumption, and the copyright protections of cinematic films.**

Section 5: Let's Save and Protect Cinema On all Devices and Applications
By Applying the *Cinema 3-Step Solution*
**After Applying the *Cinema 3-Step Solution* on Cellphones,**

**After Applying the *Cinema 3-Step Solution* on Cellphones.**

**Step 1:** Step 1 provides the consumer with the freedom, ability, and choice to access, watch, consume, and enjoy a film on a cellphone in its original contents and original aspect ratio (4:3-16:9) (Step 1). Step 1 should be a basic right of freedom and copyrights, for it should be a basic right of freedom in a democracy to have the ability to watch a movie on a phone in its original contents and original aspect ratio without the movie being cropped/visually censored by 50% or distorted/junked/morphed/composted to be nearly 50% less in size at the vertical length.

**Step 2:** Step 2 provides the consumer the freedom, ability, and choice to crop/visually censor a film on a cellphone by nearly 50% "Zoom to Fill Cellphone Screen's Aspect Ratio (19:9-21:9)" (which crops/censors the movie by nearly 50% at the top and bottom of the film).

**Step 3:** Step 3 provides the consumer the freedom, ability, and choice to distort/junk/morph/compost a film on a cellphone to be nearly 50% less in size (vertically) "Distort to Fit Cellphone Screen's Aspect Ratio (19:9-21:9)". **Bargain DVD Players and DVD player applications apply the principles of the Cinema 3-Step Solution, so there is no excuse for Hollywood, Bollywood, South Indian Cinema, Official Youtube Movie Channels, and Movie Streaming Companies like Netflix, Hulu, Prime Video, and Tubi to continue to deny the consumer and the global citizen of the most basic rights of freedom of media consumption and copyright protection on cellphones.**

## Section 5:
## Let's Save and Protect Cinema On all Devices and Applications
## By Applying the *Cinema 3-Step Solution*
## (Before)
**The Cropping, Distortion, and Visual Censorship of Cinema on Tablets Initiated by Movie Streaming Companies such as Netflix, Prime Video, Tubi, Hulu, and Official YouTube Movie Channels...**

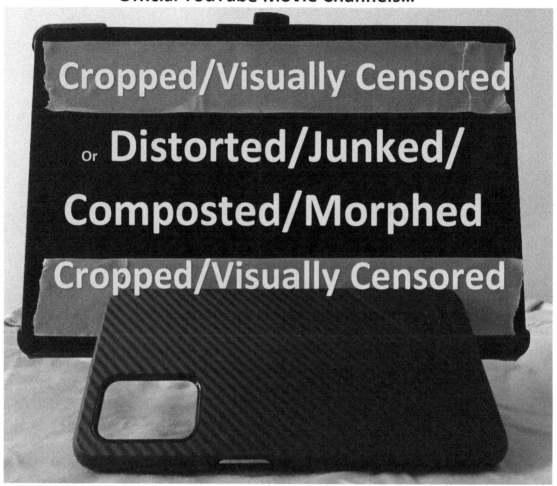

At the time of writing this page, Movie Streaming Companies like Netflix, Hulu, Prime Video, Tubi, and official YouTube Movie Channels like Shemaroo, YouTube Movies, Ultra Movie Parlour, and Goldmines force the consumers to watch the majority of all films ever created either cropped/visually censored by 50% on tablets (and all devices) or distorted, morphed, junked, and composted by 50% to be 50% less in size vertically.

Movie streaming companies <u>do not</u> provide you with the ability, freedom, and choice to consume and enjoy cinematic movies on tablets (and all devices) in their original contents & original aspect ratios.

**These are blatant violations of freedom, freedom of media consumption, and the copyright protections of cinematic films.**

Section 5:
Let's Save and Protect Cinema On all Devices and Applications
By Applying the *Cinema 3-Step Solution*
**After Applying the *Cinema 3-Step Solution on Tablets***

The *Cinema 3-Step Solution*

**Step 1:** Watch a Film in its Original Contents and Original Aspect Ratio (4:3-16:9)

**Step 2:** Watch a Film Cropped/Visually Censored "Zoom to Fit Cellphone Aspect Ratio (19:9-21:9)" (which crops/censors the movie by nearly 50% (top&bottom) of the film)

**Step 3:** Watch a Film Distorted/Junked/Morphed/ Composted "Distort to Fit Cellphone Aspect Ratio (19:9-21:9)" ((which distorts/junks/composts/morphs the movie to be nearly 50% less in size (vertically))

**After Applying the *Cinema 3-Step Solution* on tablets**

**Step 1:** Step 1 provides the consumer with the freedom, ability, and choice to access, watch, consume, and enjoy a film on a tablet in its original contents and original aspect ratio (4:3-16:9) (Step 1). Step 1 should be a basic right of freedom and copyrights, for it should be a basic right of freedom in a democracy to have the ability to watch a movie on a tablet in its original contents and original aspect ratio without the movie being cropped/visually censored by 50% or distorted/junked/morphed/composted to be nearly 50% less in size at the vertical length.

**Step 2:** Step 2 provides the consumer the freedom, ability, and choice to crop/visually censor a film on a tablet by nearly 50% "Zoom to Fit Cellphone Screen Aspect Ratio (19:9-21:9)" (which crops/censors the movie by nearly 50% at the top and bottom of the film).

**Step 3:** Step 3 provides the consumer the freedom, ability, and choice to distort/junk/morph/compost a film on a tablet nearly 50% less in size (vertically) "Distort to Fit Cellphone Screen Aspect Ratio (19:9-21:9)". **Bargain DVD Players and DVD player applications apply the principles of the Cinema 3-Step Solution, so there is no excuse for Hollywood, Bollywood, South Indian Cinema, Youtube Movie Channels, and Movie Streaming Companies like Netflix, Hulu, Prime Video, and Tubi to continue to deny the consumer/global citizen of the most basic rights of freedom of media consumption and copyright protection on tablets.**

# Section 5:
Let's Save and Protect Cinema On all Devices and Applications
By Applying the *Cinema 3-Step Solution*
**(Before)**
**The Cropping, Distortion, and Visual Censorship of Cinema on Laptops Initiated by Movie Streaming Companies such as Netflix, Prime Video, Tubi, Hulu and Official YouTube Movie Channels...**

At the time of writing this page,
Movie Streaming Companies like Netflix, Hulu, Prime Video, Tubi, and official YouTube Movie Channels like Shemaroo, YouTube Movies, Ultra Movie Parlour, and Goldmines force the consumers to watch the majority of all films ever created either cropped/visually censored by 50% on laptops (and all devices) or distorted, morphed, junked, and composted by 50% to be 50% less in size vertically.

Movie streaming companies <u>do not</u> provide you with the ability, freedom, and choice to consume and enjoy cinematic movies on laptops (and all devices) in their original contents & original aspect ratios.

**These are blatant violations of freedom, freedom of media consumption, and the copyright protections of cinematic films.**

Section 5: Let's Save and Protect Cinema On all Devices and Applications
By Applying the *Cinema 3-Step Solution*
**After Applying the *Cinema 3-Step Solution on Laptops***

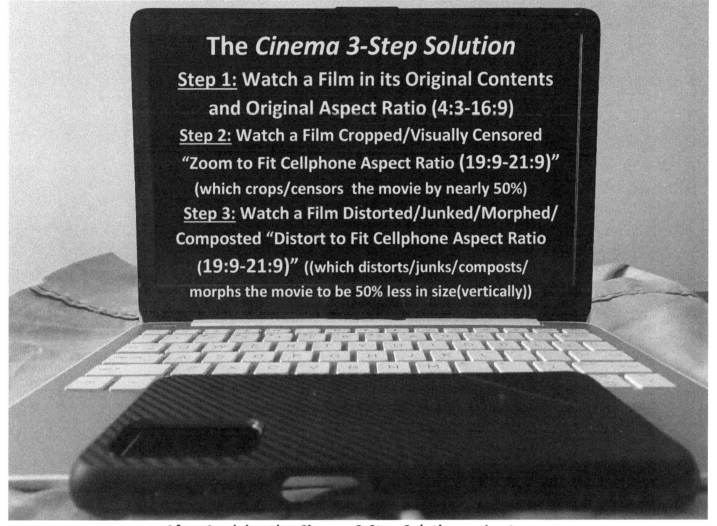

The *Cinema 3-Step Solution*
<u>Step 1</u>: Watch a Film in its Original Contents and Original Aspect Ratio (4:3-16:9)
<u>Step 2</u>: Watch a Film Cropped/Visually Censored "Zoom to Fit Cellphone Aspect Ratio (19:9-21:9)" (which crops/censors the movie by nearly 50%)
<u>Step 3</u>: Watch a Film Distorted/Junked/Morphed/ Composted "Distort to Fit Cellphone Aspect Ratio (19:9-21:9)" ((which distorts/junks/composts/ morphs the movie to be 50% less in size(vertically))

**After Applying the *Cinema 3-Step Solution* on Laptops**

<u>**Step 1:**</u> Step 1 provides the consumer with the freedom, ability, and choice to access, watch, consume, and enjoy a film on a laptop in its original contents and original aspect ratio (4:3-16:9) (Step 1). Step 1 should be a basic right of freedom and copyrights, for it should be a basic right of freedom in a democracy to have the ability to watch a movie on a laptop in its original contents and original aspect ratio without the movie being cropped/visually censored by 50% or distorted/junked/morphed/composted to be nearly 50% less in size at the vertical length.

<u>**Step 2:**</u> Step 2 provides the consumer the freedom, ability, and choice to crop/visually censor a film on a laptop by nearly 50% "Zoom to Fit Cellphone Screen Aspect Ratio (19:9-21:9)" (which crops/censors the movie by nearly 50% at the top and bottom of the film).

<u>**Step 3:**</u> Step 3 provides the consumer the freedom, ability, and choice to distort/junk/morph/compost a film on a laptop nearly 50% less in size (vertically) "Distort to Fit Cellphone Screen Aspect Ratio (19:9-21:9)". **Bargain DVD Players and DVD player applications apply the principles of the Cinema 3-Step Solution, so there is no excuse for Hollywood, Bollywood, South Indian Cinema, Youtube Movie Channels, and Movie Streaming Companies like Netflix, Hulu, Prime Video, and Tubi to continue to deny the consumer and global citizen of the most basic rights of freedom of media consumption and copyright protection on laptops.**

# Section 5:
## Let's Save and Protect Cinema On all Devices and Applications
### By Applying the *Cinema 3-Step Solution*
**(Before)**
**The Cropping, Distortion, and Visual Censorship of Cinema on Desktop Monitors Initiated by Movie Streaming Companies such as Netflix, Prime Video, Tubi, Hulu, and Official YouTube Movie Channels...**

At the time of writing this page,

Movie Streaming Companies like Netflix, Hulu, Prime Video, Tubi, and official YouTube Movie Channels like Shemaroo, YouTube Movies, Ultra Movie Parlour, and Goldmines force the consumers to watch the majority of all films ever created either cropped/visually censored by 50% on Desktop Monitors (and all devices) or distorted, morphed, junked, and composted by 50% to be 50% less in size vertically.

Movie streaming companies <u>do not</u> provide you with the ability, freedom, and choice to consume and enjoy cinematic movies on PC Monitors (and all devices) in their original contents & aspect ratios.

**These are blatant violations of freedom, freedom of media consumption, and the copyright protections of cinematic films.**

Section 5: Let's Save and Protect Cinema On all Devices and Applications
By Applying the *Cinema 3-Step Solution*
**After Applying the *Cinema 3-Step Solution* on Desktop Monitors**

## The *Cinema 3-Step Solution*

**Step 1:** Watch a Film in its Original Contents and Original Aspect Ratio (4:3-16:9)

**Step 2:** Watch a Film Cropped/Visually Censored "Zoom to Fit Cellphone Aspect Ratio (19:9-21:9)" (which crops/censors the movie by nearly 50% at the top and bottom)

**Step 3:** Watch a Film Distorted/Junked/Morphed/Composted "Distort to Fit Cellphone Aspect Ratio (19:9-21:9)" ((which distorts/junks/morphs the movie to be 50% less in size (vertically))

**After Applying the *Cinema 3-Step Solution* on Desktop Monitors**

 **Step 1:** Step 1 provides the consumer with the freedom, ability, and choice to access, watch, consume, and enjoy a film on a desktop monitor in its original contents and original aspect ratio (4:3-16:9) (Step 1). Step 1 should be a basic right of freedom and copyrights, for it should be a basic right of freedom in a democracy to have the ability to watch a movie on a desktop monitor in its original contents and original aspect ratio without the movie being cropped/visually censored by 50% or distorted/junked/morphed/composted to be nearly 50% less in size at the vertical length.

 **Step 2:** Step 2 provides the consumer the freedom, ability, and choice to crop/visually censor a film on a desktop monitor by nearly 50% "Zoom to Fit Cellphone Screen Aspect Ratio (19:9-21:9)" (which crops/censors the movie by nearly 50% at the top and bottom of the film).

 **Step 3:** Step 3 provides the consumer the freedom, ability, and choice to distort/junk/morph/compost a film on a desktop monitor by nearly 50% less in size (vertically) "Distort to Fit Cellphone Screen Aspect Ratio (19:9-21:9)". **Bargain DVD Players and DVD player applications apply the principles of the Cinema 3-Step Solution, so there is no excuse for Hollywood, Bollywood, South Indian Cinema, YouTube Movie Channels, and Movie Streaming Companies like Netflix, Hulu, Prime Video, and Tubi to continue to deny the consumer of the most basic rights of freedom of media consumption and copyright protection on desktop monitors.**

## Section 5:
Let's Save and Protect Cinema On all Devices and Applications
By Applying the *Cinema 3-Step Solution*
**(Before)**
**The Cropping, Distortion, and Visual Censorship of Cinema on Television Initiated by Movie Streaming Companies such as Netflix, Prime Video, Tubi, Hulu, and Official YouTube Movie Channels...**

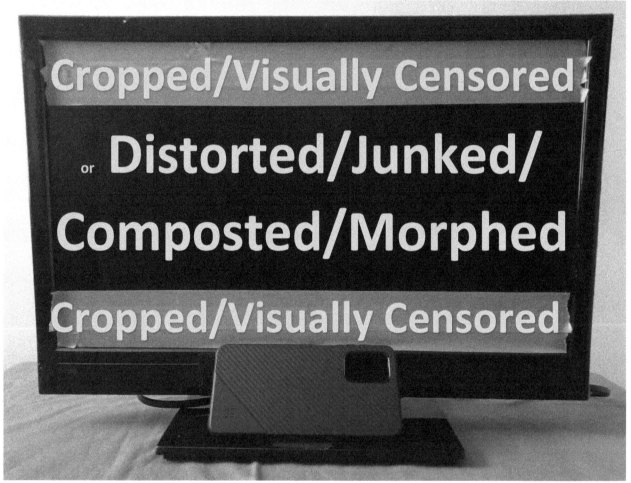

At the time of writing this page,

Movie Streaming Companies like Netflix, Hulu, Prime Video, Tubi, and official YouTube Movie Channels like Shemaroo, Ultra Movie Parlour, and Goldmines force the consumers to watch the majority of all films ever created either cropped/visually censored by 50% on televisions (and all devices) or distorted, morphed, junked, and composted by 50% to be 50% less in size vertically. Movie streaming companies <u>do not</u> provide you with the ability, freedom, and choice to consume and enjoy cinematic movies on televisions (and all devices) in their original contents & original aspect ratios.

**These are blatant violations of freedom, freedom of media consumption, and the copyright protections of cinematic films.**

Section 5: Let's Save and Protect Cinema On all Devices and Applications
By Applying the *Cinema 3-Step Solution*
**After Applying the *Cinema 3-Step Solution* on Televisions**

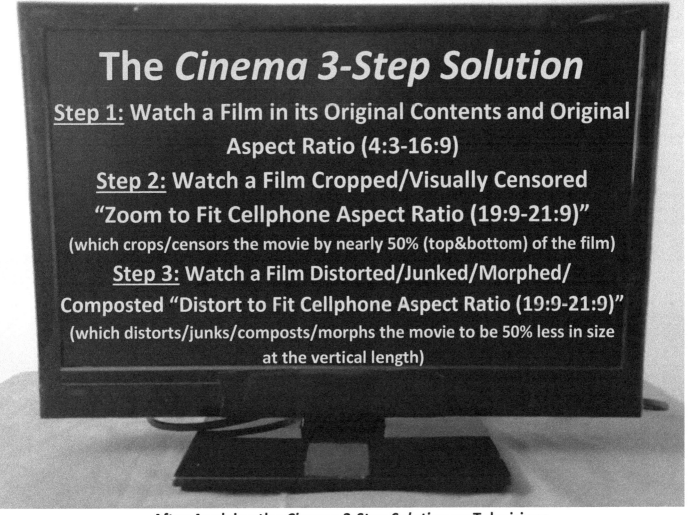

**After Applying the *Cinema 3-Step Solution* on Televisions**

**Step 1:** Step 1 provides the consumer with the freedom, ability, and choice to access, watch, consume, and enjoy a film on a Television in its original contents and original aspect ratio (4:3-16:9) (Step 1). Step 1 should be a basic right of freedom and copyrights, for it should be a basic right of freedom in a democracy to have the ability to watch a movie on a Television in its original contents and original aspect ratio without the movie being cropped/visually censored by 50% or distorted/junked/morphed/composted to be nearly 50% less in size at the vertical length.

**Step 2:** Step 2 provides the consumer the freedom, ability, and choice to crop/visually censor a film on a Television by nearly 50% "Zoom to Fit Cellphone Screen Aspect Ratio (19:9-21:9)" (which crops/censors the movie by nearly 50% at the top and bottom of the film).

**Step 3:** Step 3 provides the consumer the freedom, ability, and choice to distort/junk/morph/compost a film on a Television by nearly 50% less in size (vertically) "Distort to Fit Cellphone Screen Aspect Ratio (19:9-21:9)". **Bargain DVD Players and DVD player applications apply the principles of the Cinema 3-Step Solution, so there is no excuse for Hollywood, Bollywood, South Indian Cinema, YouTube Movie Channels, and Movie Streaming Companies like Netflix, Hulu, Prime Video, and Tubi to continue to deny the consumer/global citizen of the most basic rights of freedom of media consumption and copyright protection on Televisions.**

Section 5: Let's Save and Protect Cinema On all Devices and Applications
By Applying the *Cinema 3-Step Solution*
**Cellphones - Before and After Applying the Cinema 3-Step Solution - Photos Comparisons:**

Section 5:Let's Save and Protect Cinema On all Devices and Applications
By Applying the *Cinema 3-Step Solution*
**Laptops - Before and After Applying the Cinema 3-Step Solution - Photos Comparisons:**

Section 5: Let's Save and Protect Cinema On all Devices and Applications
By Applying the *Cinema 3-Step Solution*
**Tablets - Before and After the Cinema 3-Step Solution - Photos Comparisons:**

**How Cellphones Cropped, Distorted, and Visually Censored Cinema: Let's Save Cinema Page 103**
Section 5: Let's Save and Protect Cinema On all Devices and Applications
By Applying the *Cinema 3-Step Solution*
**Desktop Monitors - Before and After Applying the Cinema 3-Step Solution - Photos Comparisons:**

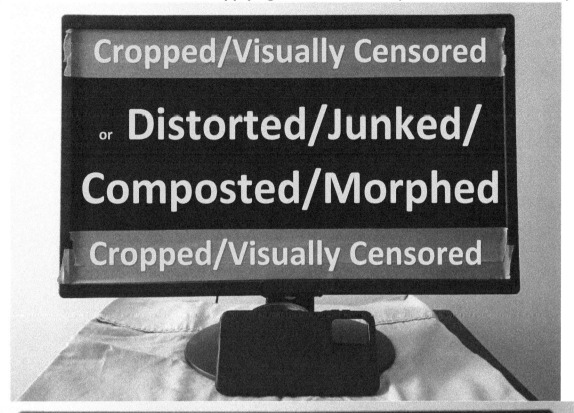

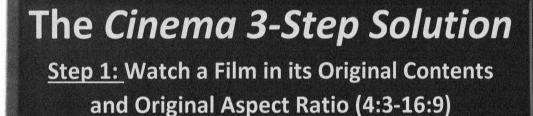

Section 5: Let's Save and Protect Cinema On all Devices and Applications
By Applying the *Cinema 3-Step Solution*
**Televisions - Before and After Applying the Cinema 3-Step Solution - Photos Comparisons:**

## Section 5:

## Let's Save and Protect Cinema On all Devices and Applications

By Applying the *Cinema 3-Step Solution* and providing the consumer and global citizen with the most basic rights of freedom, freedom of media consumption, freedom of speech, and protection of copyrights. The freedom, ability, and choice to access, consume, and enjoy a cinematic film across all devices without the film being cropped/visually censored (by nearly 50%) or distorted/junked/morphed/composted (to be nearly 50% less in size) should be a basic right of freedom, freedom of media speech, and copyright protection.


End Of Section 5. Use this page to take notes on Section 5.

# End Of Book Conclusion

Through cinema we can unite, forget our differences, relax, and enjoy amazing cinematic productions. The most basic ability to watch and experience cinema is in a dire state of visual cropping/censorship in which almost 50% percent of nearly every movie's contents ever made has been visually cropped/censored from the experience or significantly distorted/junked/composted to be 50% less in size at the vertical length. I believe that all it takes to solve this problem is education and awareness of the *Cinema 3-Step Solution* which provides the consumer the freedom, ability, and choice to watch films in their original contents & original aspect ratios (Step 1), to  visually crop/censor films "fill to zoom cellphone aspect ratio" (Step 2), or to distort/junk/compost/morph films "distort to fit cellphone aspect ratio" on their devices' screens (Step 3). One thing is for certain, the *Cinema 3-Step Solution* is very viable, as most affordable DVD players and DVD playing applications already apply the principles of the *Cinema 3-Step Solution*.

In the modern world, we do not have the freedom of media consumption to watch and enjoy movies in their original creations without nearly half of the experiences visually cropped/censored by nearly 50% or distorted/junked/composted by nearly 50%. We are denied from enjoying the emotions of love, happiness, comedy, excitement, laughter and many other emotions and experiences that can be enjoyed from watching cinematic films, as the world's films are either visually cropped/censored by 50% or visually distorted/junked/morphed/composted by 50% to be 50% less in size. These amazing emotions which we are capable of experiencing through cinematic movies are being robbed and denied all across the world by nearly 50%. I find this violation against freedom a massive failure of Hollywood, Bollywood, South Indian Cinema, Netflix, Hulu, Prime Video, Tubi, YouTube movie channels, and government agencies which seek to uphold basic principles of copyright protection and freedom of media consumption.

Freedom, Freedom of speech, copyright protection, and freedom of media consumption should apply to the worlds of cinematic films which allow us to experience and escape into Hollywood, Bollywood, and many other genres of cinematic worlds. The movie streaming world like Netflix, Hulu, Prime Video, Tubi, and YouTube movie channels continue to deny humanity the freedom, ability, and choice to access and enjoy cinematic movies in their original contents & original aspect ratios and force consumers to watch cinematic movies either visually cropped/censored by 50% or distorted/junked/composted to be 50% less in size.

One of the major benefits of life, is that life can be enjoyed, and cinema, when produced in life-like aspect ratios which simulate how the anatomical human eyes see and experience field of vision and sight in real life (the 16:9 to 4:3 aspect ratios) is arguably the best pastime in the world to enjoy life with family, friends, or by oneself. It is heartbreaking to know that movie streaming companies like Hulu, Prime Video, Netflix, Tubi, and Hollywood and Bollywood companies unite together in one common cause to deny consumers all around the world of basic human rights of freedom and freedom of media consumption across all platforms, applications, and devices. Considering how small teams of developers created bargain DVD players and bargain DVD player applications that provide and comply with the principles of freedom, freedom of media speech, and copyright protection, there is no reason for the movie streaming world of Netflix, Hulu, Prime Video, Tubi, and YouTube Movie Channels to continue to deny consumers the same basic rights of freedom & and freedom of media consumption that every human deserves.

# End Of Book Conclusion continued…

Movie streaming companies such Netflix, Hulu, Prime Video, Tubi, Hollywood, South Indian Cinema, and Bollywood companies have not only visually censored/cropped and distorted/junked/composted the world's films by 50%, but also create new content in ultrawide cellphone-aspect ratios of 19:9-21:9. It is a well-established fact that cinematic films both natively made, visually censored/cropped, or distorted to the ultrawide cellphone-aspect ratios of 19:9-21:9 at the scientific level of human sight provide non-entertaining, non-immersive, non-euphoric, and non-simulative cinematic experiences.

The limited and non-enjoyable experience of 19:9-21:9 aspect ratio films originates from the fact that those aspect ratios simulate only about 50% of the field of view of the standard field of vision & sight of the human eyes. Cinematic movies presented in the ultra-wide aspect ratios of 19:9-21:9 are in fact contraindicative to the very definition of the word "cinema". The 19:9-21:9 aspect ratios only simulate about 50% of the field of view our eyes experience sight and vision in real life, and as a result our minds can tell what is real and what is not real. The visual euphoria, visual simulation, and visual immersion of cinema does not occur from cinematic movies displayed in the cellphone aspect ratios of 19:9-21:9, for the brain can tell that the field of vision of 19:9-21:9 aspect ratio films are completely different, reduced, and significantly limited in comparison to the standard field of vision & sight of the human eyes at the scientific anatomical level.

*'Cinematic films displayed in the 16:9-4:3 aspect ratios activate and simulate the standard workings of the average human eye's aspect ratio of vision (or field of vision) which causes a visually euphoric, simulative, immersive, and enjoyable cinematic experience into cinematic worlds. The standard vision of the human eye sees and experiences life in an aspect ratio (or field of view) somewhere between the 16:9 and 4:3 aspect ratios. When we watch cinema that is also in the same aspect ratio of the standard human vision (16:9 – 4:3 aspect ratios), immersion, simulation, euphoria, and an enjoyable cinematic experience occurs.'*

The one realm of digital media which provides positive journeys, emotions, experiences, and escapes into other worlds with friends, family, and by one's self is either censored/cropped by 50% or visually distorted, junked, composted, and reduced in size by nearly 50% less at the vertical length. As a society, we are trapped in a state of cinematic cropping/visual censorship and distortion/junking/composting of cinema. We must apply efforts and take a stand for freedom, freedom of speech, and freedom of media consumption toward the most basic human right of being able to enjoy this planet's cinematic films in their original contents & original aspect ratios. Movie streaming companies such as Netflix, Hulu, Tubi, Prime Video, and Youtube Movie channels are actively and systematically visually cropping/censoring or distorting/junking/composting every cinematic movie ever made and changing the cinematic experience into an anti-cinematic, anti-consumer, non-immersive, non-simulative, non-euphoric, and non-enjoyable experience for no other reason than "fitting in" with the domino effect of mobile trends. It is important to clarify once again that mobile trends should not give movie streaming companies the right to deny consumers freedom & freedom of media consumption by actively cropping/censoring films by 50% or distorting/junking/morphing/composting films by 50% to be 50% less in size.

# End Of Book Conclusion continued...

In the modern world, no matter what continent you are on, you have no way to escape, enjoy, and to experience the joys, emotions, immersions, simulations, and experiences of cinema without nearly half of each film's content either visually cropped/censored or significantly distorted, junked, and composted from the film's original contents, original aspect ratio, and original experience.

Every moment in life is an opportunity to experience, to escape, and to enter cinematic worlds in their original contents & original aspect ratios without the visual cropping/censorship or distortion/junking/composting of cinema by nearly 50% percent. It should be a basic right of freedom, freedom of media consumption, and copyright protection to access, enjoy, and watch a film in its original contents and original aspect ratio.

The key to cinematic entertainment, immersion, simulation, visual euphoria, escapes, and experiences to enjoy cinema primarily depends on the aspect ratios which the films are made and presented in. Creating and showing films in the aspect ratios which we experience field of vision & sight in real life (between the 16:9-4:3 aspect ratios) is the key method to creating enjoyable cinematic experiences. Cinematic films presented in the 4:3-16:9 aspect ratios are the keys to experiencing life-like enjoyable, simulative, and immersive cinematic experiences. The scientific anatomical answer to the question of what aspect ratios produces the best immersions, experiences, euphorias, and escapes is within us. We experience field of vision & sight in life in between the 16:9-4:3 aspect ratios, so why as a society, are we not provided the opportunity and freedom to experience cinema the way we experience life in. At the scientific level, the 19:9 to 21:9 aspect ratios are limited non-realistic, non-immersive, non-simulative, non-euphoric, and non-enjoyable experiences. The 16:9-4:3 aspect ratios at the scientific anatomical level of the human eyes, cause the highest quality simulations, immersions, entertainments, visual euphorias, and enjoyments of the cinematic experience. The solution to happiness, meanings, escapes, emotions, and journeys in life from cinematic movies lies within the aspect ratios which we watch cinema and the field of vision of our eyes. Movie streaming companies continue to deny consumers of the most basic rights of freedom & freedom of media consumption, and they continue to deny consumers of amazing journeys and visual experiences by forcing consumers to watch movies either visually cropped/censored by 50% or visually distorted/morphed/junked/composted by 50%

*I believe that all it takes is one actor/actress or director/crew member from Hollywood, South Indian Cinema, or Bollywood to speak and raise awareness of the visual censorship/cropping and distortion/junking/morphing/composting of cinema that Hollywood, Bollywood, South Indian Cinema, Netflix, Hulu, Prime Video, Tubi, YouTube Movie channels, and other movie streaming companies have initiated.*

*It is time to end the forced visual cropping and censorship of cinema...*

*It is time to end the forced visual distortion, junking, and composting of cinema...*

*Honor Freedom, Honor Freedom of Media Consumption, Honor Copyrights*

# Let's Save and Protect Cinema on **Netflix**

# Let's Save and Protect Cinema on **Hulu**

# Let's Save and Protect Cinema on **Prime Video**

# Let's Save and Protect Cinema on **Tubi**

# Let's Save and Protect Cinema on **Youtube Movie Channels** (Shemaroo, Goldmines, YouTube Movies, Ultra Movie Parlor, and all Official Movie Channels

# Let's Save and Protect Cinema Across All Devices, Applications, and Platforms by Applying:
# The *Cinema 3-Step Solutions*

# Let's Save and Protect Cinema
# Across all Devices,
# Applications,
# and Platforms
# by Applying:

## The *Cinema 3-Step Solution*

# The End.

## The solution is simple

# The *Cinema 3-Step Solution.*

Congratulations!

You studied the entirety of this educational book.

I am grateful and appreciative that you took the time to read this book.

**I will make sure to use a portion of the profits generated from this book toward giving entirely free hardcover copies of this book to actors/actresses, directors, crew members, Bollywood companies, Hollywood companies, South Indian Cinema companies, Movie Streaming companies, and many more from the cinematic community. Every free book that I give to the cinematic community, will include a handwritten acknowledgement that the free book was funded by you, the reader. I appreciate the time and effort you applied to read this book, thanks again.**

Please enjoy the remainder of this book as I provide my final closing messages.

The End.

**Painter: KAYAMAN**

*...There are more benefits to cinematic films presented in the 4:3-16:9 aspect ratios then the number of stars able to be seen on a clear night's vision...*

... Sight (4:3-16:9) + Screens (4:3-16:9) = Visual Euphoria, Immersion, and Simulation of Cinema (an enjoyable experience) ...

... Sight (4:3-16:9) + Screens (19:9-21:9) = No Euphoria, No Immersion, and No Simulation of Cinema (a non-enjoyable experience) ...

*...The key to enjoy the visual experience of cinema is to watch cinema the way our eyes experience sight, field of views, and field of vision in real life...*

There is no greater hobby in the world then being immersed and simulated in euphoric cinematic films & shows which are presented in the aspect ratios that simulate the standard field of vision of sight (the 4:3-16:9 aspect ratios).

**Painter: KAYAMAN**

Through cinematic films presented in the aspect ratios that simulate the standard sight of the human eyes (4:3-16:9), we can escape the confides of this planet and enjoy other cinematic worlds.

The End: Closure

**Painter: KAYAMAN**
Honor Freedom
Honor Freedom of Media Consumption
Honor the Copyrights of Cinematic Films

Across All Devices, Applications, and Platforms
By Providing the Consumer and the Global Citizen with basic rights of freedom and the freedom, ability, and choice to access, consume, and enjoy films in their original contents & original aspect ratios without the films being cropped/censored by nearly 50% or distorted/junked/morphed/composted to be nearly 50% less in size at the vertical length.

The End: Closure

One of the benefits of life is that life can be enjoyed…

Happiness, purpose, and meaning in life can easily be found through accessing, consuming, watching, and enjoying cinematic films presented in field of views (or aspect ratios) which simulate the standard sight, vision, and field of view of the human eyes (the 4:3-16:9 aspect ratios). The aspect ratio of a film is the window into experiencing the cinematic world.

Cinematic movies must be restored, preserved, and protected across the world in the same way that copyrighted paintings are protected. Hollywood, Bollywood, South Indian Cinema, Official YouTube Movie Channels, and Movie Streaming Companies (like Netflix, Hulu, Prime Video Video, Tubi) must provide the global consumer and global citizen with basic rights of freedom & freedom of media consumption. It is a blatant failure and violation of freedom & copyright protections to forcefully and unnecessarily crop/visually censor films by nearly 50%. It is also a blatant failure and violation of freedom & copyright protections to forcefully and unnecessarily distort/junk/morph/compost cinematic movies to be nearly 50% less in size.

By Applying the *Cinema 3-Step Solution* to all movie streaming applications and devices, the consumer and the global citizen is provided with the most basic of human rights of freedom of media consumption to access, consume, and enjoy cinematic movies in their original contents & original aspect ratios (Step 1), cropped/visually censored by nearly 50% "zoom to fill cellphone's screen" (Step 2), or distorted/junked/composted to be nearly 50% less in size "distort to fit cellphone's screen" (Step 3).

The principles of the *Cinema 3-Step Solution* are already applied on bargain DVD players and DVD player applications, so there is no excuse or reason that Hollywood, Bollywood, South Indian Cinema, Official Youtube Movie Channels, and movie streaming applications (like Netflix, Hulu, Prime Video Video, and Tubi) to continue to violate the most basic human rights of freedom, freedom of media consumption and copyrights.

## The End: Closure:

**Painter: KAYAMAN**

Through Cinema we can put aside our different beliefs and opinions and escape the confides of this planet by enjoying cinematic films which simulate the standard sight and of field of view of the human eyes (the 4:3-16:9 aspect ratios). Through accessing, consuming, and watching cinematic films which simulate the standard field of vision of the human eyes (the 4:3-16:9 aspect ratios), visual euphoria, visual immersion, and visual simulation occurs. If we put aside our differences in opinions and beliefs of this world, we can unite to promote a world which provides all humans with basic human rights of freedom of media consumption to enjoy cinematic movies in their original contents & original aspect ratios. Everyone deserves to experience, live, and enjoy cinematic films to the max, in their original contents and original aspect ratios across all devices for happiness, purpose, excitement, meaning, escapes, and relaxation in life. One of the benefits of life is that life can be enjoyed: providing the consumer and global citizen with basic human rights of freedom of media consumption is a critical step that must be taken to ensure that humans can be happy and enjoy cinema in life.

**Let's Save Cinema**

# How Cellphones Cropped, Distorted, and Visually Censored Cinema:

# Let's Save Cinema

# Credits:

Author & Photographer: Thecyclecasenumber Goalinventionsystemauthor

## Painter: KAYAMAN

Bonus Story:

# The Quest of the Visual Euphoria, Immersion, and Simulation of Cinema

Through 6 years from 2010-2016, I pursued most of my time and efforts toward enjoying and experiencing cinema. During that time, I developed and discovered many discoveries which benefited and improved the visual euphorias, immersions, and simulations of cinematic movies and shows. There were several techniques and discoveries which I developed from 2010-2016 when I enjoyed thousands of movies (primarily Bollywood) before they were cropped, distorted, and visually censored by movie streaming companies like Netflix, Hulu, Prime Video, Tubi, and official YouTube movie channels like Shemaroo, Ultra Movie Parlour, Goldmines, Eros Entertainment, Rajshri and many others. In this mini story, I will chronicle all the techniques, tricks, and lessons that I learned from those 6 years.

From 2010-2016, I watched movies in their original contents & original aspect ratios (4:3-16:9 aspect ratios). At the time, I had no idea that after 2016, Netflix, Hulu, Prime Video, Tubi and official Youtube Movie channels like Shemaroo, Ultra Movie Parlour, and Goldmines would crop/visually censor films by 50% or distort/junk/morph/compost films by 50% to be 50% less in size vertically. During those 6 years, I could never have predicted that cinema would be cropped, distorted, and visually censored by movie streaming companies like Netflix, Hulu, Prime Video, Tubi, and Official YouTube movie channels whose jobs it is to provide consumers movies and shows to consume, access, and enjoy.

After the cropping, distortion, and visual censorship performed by movie streaming companies, I quickly realized that watching movies in their original contents and in their original aspect ratios which simulate the standard field of vision of the human eyes (the 4:3-16:9 aspect ratios) is the most important factor, science, and method to enjoy the visual euphorias, immersions, and simulations of cinemas. Within days of the first cropping, distortion, and visual censorship of cinema initially initiated by Netflix, my heart was broken to see that all my favorite movies' contents and experiences were cropped, distorted, and visually censored. When I thought about the current generation not being provided basic human rights of freedom, freedoms of speech, and freedoms of media consumption to enjoy films without them being cropped, distorted, or visually censored, I was inspired to create this book, *How Cellphones Cropped, Distorted, and Visually Censored Cinema*. For years until 2022, I would witness platforms, applications, and channels needlessly and unnecessarily deny consumers and global citizens basic rights of copyrights, freedom, and freedom of media consumption, by cropping/visually censoring films by 50% or distorting/junking/morphing/composting films by 50% to be 50% less in size. By far, the most important science, factor, and method to enjoy cinematic movies and shows is to watch them in their original aspect ratios (the 4:3-16:9) which simulate the standard field of vision of sight and the human eyes.

The second most important science, factor, and method to enjoy cinema is to savor the cinematography, the scenery, the colors, and all the objects in movies and shows. After several years, I discovered that cinematic movies and shows provide great inspiration and thought. I termed this phenomenon of transferring the visual scenery of cinema to thoughts as "Cinema Invention". The ability to watch cinematic movies and shows and think about ideas, reflect, and ponder is truly amazing.

Bonus Story:

# The Quest of the Visual Euphoria, Immersion, and Simulation of Cinema

After learning the techniques of performing the process of transferring watching the visual scenes of cinema into thoughts and ideas, I quickly realized that I needed a journal nearby to write down thoughts while enjoying cinematic movies and shows. I termed this hobby as "Cinema Invention". Having a journal at the ready to write down thoughts and ideas arose as I enjoyed cinematic movies and shows added a exciting and relaxing addition to the cinematic experience. The power of the mind to perform cinema invention is truly amazing.

Another component between 2010-2016 that I discovered helped to improve the cinematic experience by improving the visual euphorias, immersions, and simulations of cinemas was to create homemade cinematic environments which removed surrounding stimuli and objects of distraction. This task was easily done by making a custom homemade curtain to create wall dividers. To create wall dividers I used simple linen bed sheets as curtains and I applied them to a homemade wooden bar which I used to create the homemade curtains. These homemade curtains were adjustable and could be easily moved to the left and right. Homemade movie curtains helped reduce the amount of distractions of external objects and stimuli and allowed me to be more immersed and simulated with the cinematic movies and shows I accessed, consumed, and watched. The homemade custom movie curtains created many improved visually euphoric experiences. I only needed to use one curtain at a time, as I used the room's wall as a natural barrier to reduce external distractions.

The final component to enjoying cinematic movies and shows is by enjoying my favorite beverages while I watched and enjoyed cinematic movies and shows.

The purpose of Cinema is to enjoy cinema by enjoying visually euphoric, visually immersive, and visually simulative cinematic experiences.

I hope you enjoyed this bonus story.

CPSIA information can be obtained
at www.ICGtesting.com
Printed in the USA
BVHW062034030622
638689BV00001B/2

9 781624 293573